GW00862956

STORIES OF THE WALLED CITY

2711	Eser:	Sur Kenti Hikayeleri
	Yazar:	Ali Ayçil
	Yayıncı:	Sterling Publishers Pvt. Ltd.
	Ülke:	Hindistan

Ali Ayçil was born in Erzincan in 1969. He completed his primary, secondary, and higher secondary education in Erzincan. He graduated from the Department of History, Kazım Karabekir Education Faculty in Erzurum Atatürk University. His poems and writings on poetry have been published in journals like *Dergâh, Hece,* and *Kitaplık*. Currently, he is the editor of the literary magazine *Dergâh*. His works include, *Arastanın Son Çırağı* (The Last Lamp of the Bazaar – poems), *Naz Bitti* (Coyness Ended – poems), *Ceviz Sandıklar ve Para Kasaları* (Walnut Chests and Safe Boxes – essays), *Kovulmuşların Evi* (House of Outcasts – essays), and *Yenilgiden Dönerken* (While Returning from Defeat – essays).

STORIES OF THE WALLED CITY

Ali Ayçil

Translated by
Dr Mohsin Ali

STERLING PUBLISHERS (P) LTD.
Regd. Office: A1/256 Safdarjung Enclave,
New Delhi-110029. Cin: U22110DL1964PTC211907
Phone: +91 82877 98380
e-mail: mail@sterlingpublishers.in
www.sterlingpublishers.in

Stories of the Walled City
© 2018 Dergah Yayinlari
Translated by Dr Mohsin Ali
Edited by Sanjiv Sarin
ISBN 978 81 944007 6 9

All rights are reserved.
No part of this publication may be reproduced, stored in a
retrieval system or transmitted, in any form or by any means,
mechanical, photocopying, recording or otherwise, without the
prior written permission of the original publisher.

Printed in India

Printed and Published by Sterling Publishers Pvt. Ltd.,
Plot No. 13, Ecotech-III, Greater Noida - 201306, U P, India

TRANSLATOR'S NOTE

The author of the book presents the epitomic lyrical beauty of the Turkish language. The book is indeed a great literary piece of artistic literature. I am conscious of this fact and have endeavoured to instil the original spirit and values into English for the readers. This translation work is a good example of doing justice with equal love and emotional attachment to both languages without compromising on the work's moral integrity and dignity.

I have attempted to inculcate similar emotions in the mind of the English reader as present in the original text. If the intensity of the beautiful and complex ideas in the Turkish text is perceived by the reader in a manner similar to the way I have been touched by it, it would be ample reward for me.

The translated Turkish stories are impervious to the style of the target literature, and bond well with their original text. The historical as well as cultural discourse of both the old and new worlds of Turkey is intricately reflected throughout the stories of Ayçil. The stories here are independent, yet interlinked to one another at the same time. The philosophy of life and the wisdom of the East are dealt with much depth and ease. The author is a master story-teller. Once you are inside the stories, everything and everyone starts to have a dialogue with you.

This work would have not been possible without Mubassir Anjum, a dear friend of mine and a connoisseur of Turkish literature and its cultural cosmology. His insights about the cultural nuances of the idioms and phrases helped me immensely to distinguish and translate the literal as well as the metaphorical undertones of the text. He remained at my side throughout the process of translation and assisted me to convey and inject the beauty of Turkish language into the work through the lucidity of English.

I hope that the readers enjoy the stories as much as I enjoyed translating them.

Dr Mohsin Ali

PREFACE

My intention was to write independent stories which were lived in the Walled City. I started writing them also. However, when I came to the story of Storyteller Tahir and had not yet written the end of the story, two protagonists came up. I was not sure whether to tell their stories – the Traveller Ibn Battuta from Tangier and the Charming Makbule. Both of them said that their beloveds were in these stories, and that I had no right to separate them from their beloveds. Later, they pointed out the almost serious mistakes I had made in the stories and offered help – if I wanted to accept. Of course, this help was to be mutual.

The Traveller from Tangier claimed that he could provide the description of the Walled City, as far as he remembered, provided he was excluded from the stories and they were told in the form of a travel book. I agreed to that. To come to an agreement with Charming Makbule proved to be much more difficult than dealing with the Traveller. She had solid information related to the stories I had already written as well as the new stories I was going to write. In order to convince her to stay with the project, many times I had to shower her with praise. Nevertheless, I cannot help but think that it was Makbule who made the most out of the situation.

Charming Makbule advised that the stories were not independent from one another as I had thought and I should consider them in the shape of a bunch of grapes. She put two conditions in front of me to show the interrelatedness between them. Firstly, I should not touch her words even a little. She would tell some things about the protagonists of her choosing and I should put them in the book as they were. Secondly, I should not tell in any way who was the man that she loved. I accepted her conditions. Despite the difficulties our agreement faced, I kept my promise to Charming Makbule and did my best to hide the identity of the man she loved.

The strange thing is that whatever both of them said came out to be true. Without even realizing it, I had written stories that could be read independently of one another and yet were related too. You cannot imagine how sad it was for me to learn that almost all the protagonists lived in the last century of the city.

Ali Ayçil

CONTENTS

	Translator's Note	v
	Preface	vii
1.	Traveller Ibn Battuta Leaves Mahinur	1
2.	Sakine's Blinded Eyes	13
3.	The Last Show of the Magician Seyfettin	18
4.	Wise Mansur Abandons the City	22
5.	The Horse with No Memories Runs Faster	26
6.	The Three Daughters of Moneylender Nizamettin	29
7.	What Hüsrev Told about Himself	34
8.	The Young Apprentice of Stableman Behram	38
9.	When the Traveller Left	42
10.	The Last Miniature of the Miniaturist Burhanettin	46
11.	Konos, the Bandit	50
12.	Muhyettin's Dry Shirt in the Rain	55
13.	The Palms of Majnun Nurettin	59
14.	The Foot in the Stirrup	63
15.	The Birdcage of Ironsmith Rifat	68
16.	The Herbalist Who Died between Laughs	72
17.	Charming Makbule	76
18.	The Cut-Off Tongue of the Storyteller Tahir	94
19.	Metaphor of the Mountain	98
20.	The Last Sight of the Imagined City	101

I took the road to see this city in vain:
to be remembered better it always had to stay the same
and stand still,
It melted, came untwined and vanished
And the World forgot it.

Italo Calvino

TRAVELLER IBN BATTUTA LEAVES MAHINUR

It had been exactly eight years, seven months and thirteen days since he left Tangier, where his mother had given birth to him, when traveller Ibn Battuta began the preparation for a new journey together with his three handmaidens in the city of Saraycik (small palace), where he last stayed. He had been on the road since he was twenty-two years old and he had lost the distance between the road and the traveller. Eight years ago, from the time he left his mother who he would never see again, until this moment, he had changed countless horses, camels, and mules. He had stayed in tents, inns, madrasas, and even in homes of people he barely knew. He had been wandering around from one city to another, the names of which he hadn't heard before. What places he had not crossed until he arrived in the powerful and esteemed town of Uzbek Han? He travelled for months on the Mediterranean coasts, the head and flies of which could swallow a man. He roamed around the ruins of the legendary library of Alexandria with sadness. He swore and cursed at the Pharaoh's tombs in Cairo. While passing through the shore of the Dead Sea, he renewed his faith by reciting Bismillah. He shed tears on the Hajar-ul Aswad, half of which was taken away by the rebels. He formed a line between the three beautiful sisters, Damascus, Baghdad, and Jerusalem. Finally, he reached Crimea through the land of the Ahi Brotherhood, who had no match in their friendship.

In all these journeys, the Traveller had countless handmaidens, each of who were bought in one city and sold in another. In all these journeys, he bandaged the wounds given by the roads with women and the wounds given by the women with roads, and had never thought about the fate of either.

Ibn Battuta remained in Uzbek Han's vast country for three months. He admired his grand tent, its colourful plume fluttering in the wind, and his soldiers, the numbers of which even Uzbek Han did not know. He visited the cities that took days and months to reach from one to the other in horse-drawn carts built just like a house. He had the opportunity to set off with the Sultan's Byzantine wife Beyelûn Hatun and even see the city of her king-father, Istanbul.

And in these lands, he encountered many new customs. He witnessed that after every meal they drank kumis, they disapproved eating sweets, they gave the heaviest punishments to horse thieves, and they held women superior to men. He was greeted by the wives of Uzbek Han – Melike, Kebek, Beyelun, and Urduca, one by one. Each of them offered gifts, better than the other, to the Traveller from Tangier. During his visits, of these four wives, he looked at Melike carefully. He understood in no time why Han loved her most and regularly went to her every evening despite the fact that she was the oldest of them all. Some nights he joined the praying session with dervishes and watched with astonishment that the dervishes finished their praying sessions mostly by playing a musical instrument. These lands were much more eye-catching than other countries, which he eagerly stepped on and abandoned. He didn't really understand how days passed until he reached Han's border city, Saraycik.

Traveller Ibn Battuta did not like border cities. These cities were full of merchants, pilgrims, and fugitives who were always on the run, and the cities would keep getting into the hands of either side in wars. They had rented two horse-drawn carriages covered with felt awnings. He had put everything needed for the journey, along with the three handmaidens, one of who was pregnant, into the carriages and prepared them completely to take the road. However, the merchants' caravan, with whom they would pass the thirty-day steppe between the cities of Saraycik and Ürgenç, wasn't ready still. At the end of four long and boring days, the wagons for the journey came to order and Ibn Battuta set off towards the human-swallowing yellow plains of the steppe with his two carts, handmaidens, and water skins filled with water.

The Traveller loved the deserts and steppes, too, if they were not exposed to bandit raids, did not run out of water and food, and did not lose their way. The sounds coming out of the caravan's water skins filled with water would mingle with the sound of the wind, and a person could travel peacefully for days on these endless plains, where every aspect of nature merged with one another in a harmonious way.

The first fifteen days of his journey passed as he hoped. For fifteen days, he listened peacefully to the sound of water coming out of the water skins without thinking about the new cities he would come across and took two breaks in the daytime. During all his breaks he filled his stomach only with the food prepared by the Greek handmaiden and smiled at the dark-skinned handmaiden with the eagerness of a man who would become a father for the first time. When it became dark, he called the handmaiden with dimples on her cheeks, who was a gift from Uzbek Han, and he did not forget to cover up all the stars with the felt awning every time. He did not even feel the freezing cold of the steppe nights thanks to the warmth of the Tatar handmaiden.

On the fifteenth day of his journey, his fate began to change suddenly, and grief sat on the gentle face of Traveller Ibn Battuta. First, he lost the dark-skinned handmaiden who gave birth in the middle of the steppe, and four days after that, he suffered heartbreak from his inability to keep his first child alive. In these harsh days when the steppe sealed his memory with two deaths, there was no one for him to take refuge in, other than the warmth of the two handmaidens, one Greek and the other Tatar. The road had become heavier for him and instead of the sounds coming out of the water skins, he had started to hear the weak screams of the dead child, which had been swallowed by the wilds. Until now, he had managed to pass three Arabian deserts and the big Desht-i Qipchaq (Cumania) without any loss, and had started this steppe journey with the same confidence. He had hoped that they would finish the journey, that started as four people, as five in Ürgenç. But the steppe and the plains of pain were not over yet. He travelled for a few more days with the sadness of the two losses, far from the knowledge that he would end the journey, that started with four people, alone.

On the twenty-seventh night of their departure, the Greek handmaiden fell ill, unable to withstand this inexhaustible wilderness, the night frosts, and the burning heat of the days. Ibn Battuta was quick to see the traces of death on the face of his handmaiden, who had a broad forehead, long eyelashes, and grief-stricken eyes. The first thing to greet him, when he was awakened by the silhouette of the mountains that appeared on the horizon on the morning of the thirtieth day, was the dead body of the patient he had come near the previous night with compassion. The other event he faced was the betrayal of the Tatar handmaiden with a slender waist, who he had left with his warmth in the other cart. The Tatar handmaiden, who had actually been dallying with the Heratian fur merchant since the beginning of the journey, disappeared that night. Finally, the thirtieth day was over. The Traveller from Tangier, wrapping the pain of three deaths in the bundle of being deceived, reached the outskirts of Ürgenç in the evening of the next day. He was all alone, helpless, and full of shame.

Traveller Ibn Battuta stayed for two days and two nights in Ürgenç, where the people swayed in the streets like a sea. Undoubtedly, he would have been amazed by this large, spectacular city if he had encountered it at another time. But his eyes, stamped by betrayal, saw nothing but an amorphous and dazzling crowd, exaggerated palaces, and unimaginative bazaars. As soon as he entered the city, he left the caravan which shared his secrets. He spent the day and the next with the trepidation of stumbling upon one of his travel companions and when it got dark, he took refuge in a small mosque instead of an inn. There he prayed in pain and talked with himself again and again. Until now, he had changed many handmaidens and seen many deaths. What could be the reason that he was suffering so much now? Every time the Traveller thought, he connected the agony in his soul with two reasons – the child and the betrayal. He understood that with the death of a child of his own, he was unable to handle the betrayal of a woman of his own at the same time.

4

Though he was tired from the journey, he spent two nights with little sleep. It was almost like it was he who woke up the birds from their sleep. And for these two long days, not knowing where he would go from there and what he would do, he roamed around from one bazaar to another. He looked like an exhausted fish hung on the fishing rod of the sun among people he did not know. He looked at the counters of the shops and exhibitions absentmindedly. He unwittingly ran down the same path several times and returned to his own life-house every time. This city was the shore of his bad luck. He wanted to go away as soon as possible. He learned from the people he asked that there was a more secluded city in the south of Ürgenç – Kat.

The heavy-hearted Traveller, who was thinking more about getting away than the city where he was going, travelled south for four days on a camel he hired. This eight-year-old traveller, who had made the roads his home, was for the first time without a guide and a caravan. He was alone with the road for the first time, although he knew of the bandits and wild animals' passion for lonely travellers. He reached Kat at noon on the fourth day without being disturbed by fear. The road eased the sorrow given by another road, and when he arrived in this new city, he could sort out the tangled ropes of his mind a little.

When he entered the city of Kat, he had only one thought – to find an inn, feed himself, bathe, and sleep. He went and settled in an inn, filled his stomach, sat on the central massage platform of the hammam and sweated for a long time, and then sat near the basin and got rid of all his dirt. Afterwards, he fell asleep in a double room that was given to him.

How could he know that when he woke up with the adhan in the morning of the next day, the shapeless man he found asleep in the next bed would determine the next course of his destiny? He woke up and while performing namaz, he could not stop himself from smiling, realizing that his roommate was snoring with the snort of a predatory animal. He must be in a deep sleep, he thought. This was the first time that he was meeting the bandit Konos, thanks to the festivity of these houses. We will never know that how much the Traveller, who stayed in the room of that inn that day and found Konos, the Bandit, sleeping in the morning, got to know Konos or how much friendship developed between the two. Konos, who left ugly marks on the face of the law, had learned years ago that one should tell no secret to the people one met. All we know is that during the five nights they stayed together, Konos told Ibn Battuta about the city he felt passionately connected to and turned the Traveller's path towards that coastal city.

To go to the Walled City, the stories of which he had listened to for five days, the Traveller from Tangier headed towards south-east again. He rode for five days through a very secluded valley. He was not impatient. He knew how to look at the city many felt attached to, from a different angle. He knew that the real city was often far from the exaggerated depictions of those who felt attached to it. Therefore, during his journey, he did not think much about how the Walled City would come out to be, but concerned himself with the state of the high valley through which he travelled. Remembering the countries, seas, deserts, and interesting stories which left traces in his memory, he took care not to leave his mind alone. He looked at the plains lying quietly over the soil and became sad. And once in a while he thought of his hometown, going back to which would take seasons. The Traveller arrived in the Walled City on the fortieth day of his departure from Saraycik. He was to do the mourning of the fortieth day of his journey of death in this city.

THE WALLED CITY

Every city has a place from where it is first seen and a moment when it is first seen. Ibn Battuta from Tangier saw the mid-sized Walled City, which was built on a plain surrounded by mountains, for the first time through a narrow gap where one curve ends and another begins, while descending from the northern slopes of the city. At that moment, he looked at it through the eyes of countless cities in his memory. With this experience, he whispered three words, hoping that he would not be mistaken – gloom, memory, death!

He saw a city that had lost its excitement. He understood this from that strange dust cloud that always covered all the exhausted cities. Every city that had lost its excitement would find solace in its memories. It would multiply its memories, deform them, reshape them, and after a while it would not be able to distinguish itself from its memories. These were the cities that talked with themselves and listened to themselves. The end of all of them was inevitable – to be remembered by their memories. Also, in such cities, the monotony of life over time coagulated some people's souls, and these coagulated souls prepared an unexpected end for their owners. Perhaps it was these immortal endings that connected Konos to this city. Or maybe, Konos was waiting for his city to give him an immortal end! Ibn Battuta was aware that when he saved his first image of the Walled City, hanging between the two folds on the slopes, in his memory and started again, he would enter a big house whose end was near.

When the Traveller entered the city at the time when the minarets were shorter than their shadows, the city was desolate. Passing through prying glances that saw the stranger either as a misled passenger or a sign of life, he reached the inn at the square. In the inn, they give him the room where the storyteller Tahir stayed. They helped him carry his belongings and arranged for him to take a bath in the adjacent hammam. They set up a delicious dinner table for him. In the evening, he was sent off to his room with respect. Numan, the owner of the inn, who had entertained countless guests, could easily see the experience and mournful traces in him. He had the nobility to hide his curiosity about the serenity of surrender in the visitor's face. Numan used to entertain every guest with what he brought. The luggage of this last guest was heavy. He realized the next day itself that he was not mistaken at all. While having his breakfast, the Traveller asked him about the population of the city, whether the governor visited the bazaar, the size of the wheat crop, the number of herbalists in the city, how many times a year iron came into the market of the iron smiths, whether there were many stray dogs, the location of the mental hospital, and who looked after the miniaturist workshop. Recording the answers in his gaze, he went out to the city.

Knowing that the squares were the summary of the cities, Seyyah started to listen to the heart of the Walled City from the square just like he did in all the cities. He took a look at the tired square surrounded by a mosque with worn stones, a market with only a few customers, a mental hospital with a wooden door cracked at several parts, three herbalists, four horseshoers, and other shops. He looked intently at the finely-gilded swords that hung on the showcase of Ironsmith Rifat. He greeted Moneylender Nizamettin, who was bargaining over a ruby ring with a female customer. He paid attention to Crazy Nurettin, who came to him smiling. He watched Horseshoer Fettan, taming a cranky foal and how skilfully he shoed it. He compared Herbalist Yusuf's fancy shop, which had countless items in it, with the similar ones he had seen before. He walked around the lifeless neighbourhoods, half of which lay in ruins, and noticed that someone from these neighbourhoods was leaving in the dirty hours of the night. He listened to the exhaustion that had settled even in the most fateful of voices. He heard the name Charming Makbule a few times coming out their mouths, mixed with laughter. He looked at the governor's palace on the west slope, whose fat of power had long melted, for a long time. And he met the man who allowed him to participate in the city's one-thousand-nine-hundred-and-sixty-nine-year history for two years – Miniaturist Burhanettin.

When Ibn Battuta finished his trip, which lasted almost thirty years, and returned to his country, he would tell Ibn Juzeyy, who helped him prepare his travel book, asking him not to record it, and passing over some parts, his arrival in the Walled City and what happened after that day:

O Ibn Juzeyy,

It wasn't Konos, the Bandit, who took me to the Walled City. His scars of torture on his face gave me a sense of gloom every time I looked at them during the five days when we stayed together. I was able to understand the emotions of this man, who was passionately attached to the city where he was born, despite the fact that he had caused its people countless fears and was cursed by them many times. Some people feel a strange kind of loyalty to the places where they have suffered. I had experienced this before I knew Konos. As you can understand, there was only one reason that made me make my way to the Walled City – betrayal. I was betrayed, O Ibn Juzeyy. Now I was also one of the countless betrayal stories I had heard in the inns I stayed in. Maybe, in one of the rough rest houses I stayed in or in a caravan that I was a part of, people would tell my story, not knowing it was about me, to pass their time. Again, as you can understand, this has nothing to do with whether we love a woman or not. No doubt, the Tatar handmaiden was beautiful, stubborn, and difficult. But I was not so embarrassed of her being the one who betrayed. Rather, I was more embarrassed about I being the one who got betrayed. I could not return to my country because it was too far to return. I couldn't join a caravan again and continue on my way, because I was unable to bear the weight of my shame. The solution I clung to was to go out of my route and find a secluded city where I could stay for a while. Konos did not divert my mind; he just spelled the name of the city that was passing through my mind.

I first saw the Walled City from the slope of a high mountain in the middle of the fifth day of my journey. It was an encounter that only multiplied my sorrow. Its appearance in the centre of the plain resembled that of a widow who was busy passing her time in her house in the middle of her sizeable garden. Even though twenty-one years have passed since then, I can still remember the three words that spilled out of my tongue when I first saw the city – gloom, memory, and death. The city sat on the first two, waiting for the third. When I arrived there in the afternoon, I found the presence of two out of my three words and signs of the third. I wasn't wrong.

I spent my first night in an inn with twenty-four rooms and four customers. This was an inn overlooking the city's square and an owner who was kind to his travellers. I washed, had food, and fell asleep. In the morning, I went out for a walk. I examined the square, greeted people, wandered around their neighbourhood, and took a look at the palace of the city. From the polished behaviour of the people and the weathered cut-stones on the walls, I understood that this city had been around for some time. Later, Miniaturist Burhanettin, who I met that day, told me that the first stone of the Walled City was put by the cruel Persian king, Zahak. He said the cruel king stayed in the city for just two summers. Later, I thought that his smell was still there in the soil of this city. Sometimes people had such strange endings.

My confidant, Ibn Juzeyy, I guess you too have sensed that my voice changes every time I remember the name Miniaturist Burhanettin. Why should it not? It was he who caused me to stay for two years in a place I had just gone with the intention of staying for two weeks. I entered the city one afternoon and it was again one afternoon that I met the Miniaturist. I had wandered around as much as I could on *that day, and decided to return to the inn to relieve my hunger and to continue the unfinished conversation with Numan. I continued on my way from a wide street that I hoped would reach the square of the city, encountering some curious looks, and some greetings. As I walked, I saw the Miniaturist walking out of a garden which had large chestnut trees hanging down the road, about ten steps ahead of me. He got out and waited for me to reach him, hoping I would accompany him until the square. We greeted each other. We met just as two strangers meet. I saw many miniatures on his face, some of which were unfinished, and he saw many roads on my face that had not yet been taken. Let's put it this way, we had faces that complemented each other's lines. The questions and answers that we asked and answered kept us occupied until the square. We separated there. He went to Moneylender Nizamettin and I went to the inn. If not that day, then the next day for sure, he came and asked for me as the short journey we made until the square together was enough to show that our destiny raised us with the same incompleteness. It happened as I expected. When I woke up in the morning, I found the Miniaturist sitting in the large courtyard of the inn. That was my last night there. The next day I settled in the house of the elderly Burhanettin, who insisted that I spend my short stay at his place.*

You also know, my brother Ibn Juzeyy, that a house can hide its secrets from a guest of two days but never from a guest of twelve days. And it couldn't. From the third day to the twelfth day, when it was time for me to go, I fell asleep and woke up with that secret, which opened itself a little more each day. I saw the quiet Mahinur, whose mother had already died, from the curtain opening of the window overlooking the garden, for the first time. Then I saw her from the gap in the door and later from the door that was open. First, I heard some small clicks in the room I was staying, then her restrained whispers, and then her voice while she watered the flowers. In this exhausted city, where I reached after travelling for five days, after the fifth day in that house, my attention shifted to Mahinur from her father the Miniaturist's words that were heavy with wisdom. I do not think that the old Burhanettin might not have understood this change in me. On the contrary, he was happy to see the silk thread that attached me to his house completely, get thicker with every passing day. Finally, when it was time for me to go, I was busy not preparing for the road, but preparing the dowry of Mahinur. Don't be surprised if everything was so short, because we do not have the knowledge to keep God's account of fates yet!

My good-hearted confidant, I'll tell you the rest of the story, too. But first, let me clarify about the suspicious question stuck in your mind. No, Mahinur was not just a whim I got tied up with so that she would heal the wound of betrayal that I had got. She had a charm which made me forget all the women I had been with and closed the door for all the women who could come in the future. I also want you to know that it was only Mahinur who could make me, whose only home was the roads, understand that I should not have any road other than the one which goes to my home. O Ibn Juzeyy, let me continue, and I hope that I have removed the suspicion in your mind.

In a short time, we complied with the custom of reaching the end of courtship. On the twenty-second day of my stay, I got married to Mahinur on the condition of continuing my stay in the same house. We were married for one full year, eleven months, and seven days. Now remembering once again her behaviour that had been diluted by custom, the lightness in her walk, the restraint in her speech, her ingenuity to make me miss her terribly, the sweetness in her gaze, and the nobility in her silence, rends my heart. No silk would look as beautiful on any woman as it did on her.

This Traveller Ibn Battuta, with whom you sit today and write his memories together with him, is a man who passed a golden strip right through the middle of his life. You just remember this. And you also should know that the essence of this sad friend of yours, sitting across you, was created for the roads. No matter how much I wanted, I was not able to thicken that gold strip enough to fill the second half of my life with it. The roads that offered me the best gift came at the end of the second year to wake up the traveller from his sleep of happiness. I started seeing Mahinur smiling in the cities I couldn't go to. The Walled City, where I met her, faded from the scene. There was an incessant fight between the cities in me and the Mahinur in me for a full month. During this time, I was weakened and my eyes got pitted. Miniaturist Burhanettin, both my friend and my father-in-law, was quick to feel the change that had started to break me off from his daughter, just as he had felt the change that attached me to his daughter in the beginning. I knew that with his trust in God, the way my father-in-law had accepted my arrival as a result of fate, he also agreed with fate taking me away.

As for Mahinur, she could feel the smallest change in me instantly, unlike any other woman. The difference between her and other women

.

11

was not her silence that she kept for one month while I was torn between her and the cities I couldn't go to, but her silence when I told her my decision to go. You know, my confidant, Ibn Juzeyy, that silence cannot be explained.

O Ibn Juzeyy, I dug my wounds up to my capacity while telling you all this. By telling you the details of my separation I do not want to go back to that day which doesn't want to break its threads attached to me at any cost. Let me tell you this much – I left a ruined young woman behind me and a secluded city that I thought would turn to ruin one day. I have no doubt that strange stories were lived after my departure, as they did before me, because in the sinking cities, people want their endings to be as loud as the city's sunset. This is not for show. Rather, it is a final attempt to make sure that one is alive. It is a pity that all traces of the stories, along with the Walled City, will be erased one day.

Now, we can continue our journey from where we left-off. After the city of Kat we travelled one more day between the vineyards, gardens, houses, and fields. Finally, we arrived at the city of Bukhara, the hometown of Abu Abdullah Muhammed Ismail Buharî, the leader of hadith scholars. This city was once the centre of the region of Amu River of Transoxiana.

2

SAKINE'S BLINDED EYES

I'm Numan.

I am the owner of both this inn and the adjoining house.

Tonight, for the first time, as there is nowhere else to go, I'm no less than a guest in my own inn. I'm a guest in one of the rooms I rent out to others. And I'm just a tired traveller on one of the beds I generally get ready for others. If it wasn't for what I've been through today, instead of sitting beside this quivering lamp, reflecting my sadness, I would now have been in deep sleep alongside my wife, Sakine. But today, my wife, Sakine, came in front of me twice – once at sunrise and once at sunset – and played a game that would condemn me to live with this pain till the day I die. Actually, I am still not sure about calling what she did a game. I have used this word just to console myself and because I have not been able to comprehend the reason for the things that have happened. In fact, when I think about my misfortune one more time by putting my thoughts together, it shows that God still has pity for me. Because I could easily be one of those people who went crazy all of a sudden and whose stories are told everywhere. If I am not crazy today, I owe it only to the mercy of my Owner. Still, I don't know whether I'll survive till the morning or not. The agony I am suffering from is not something that will go away with the rising sun. Even if I survive till morning, the darkness I have fallen into will deprive me of all the gifts that the coming days hold for me. When I tell you what I've been through, you will more than believe me that the things that I've been talking about are not just empty words.

13

Just like every day, I woke up early in the morning. Just like every morning, my wife, Sakine, had woken up before me and was busy preparing breakfast for her husband, who would go to the inn adjacent to the house. Or, at least, I was assuming so. I sank into my bed a little more, intending to extend my sleep, waiting for her to come and call me. This was my routine. I liked to stay in my bed a little more, while listening to the clatter Sakine made in the kitchen. But the signs of how this morning was going to unfold, started to emerge just as I was about to close my eyes. Somehow, I couldn't hear the clatter in the kitchen that used to come to me like a lullaby every morning. I didn't look for the reason at first. I turned to my right and then to my left and waited for the moment when my wife would come to my bedside and say, 'Get up, Numan.'

I do not know how long I waited, because when one is waiting, time tends to fold into itself, and a short moment may stretch infinitely. As the waiting prolonged, I became suspicious. After a while, that suspicion made me get up from my bed without waiting for the arrival of my wife, Sakine. I went towards the kitchen while scratching the right side of my chest. I found Sakine standing near the window and staring at the breakfast table she had laid out. She had not yet tied her hair back and some light in the shape of a circle was falling on her forehead. She was so lost that I had to search for a while for her eyes under her lovelocks and her body under her wine-coloured nightgown. It was like there was a boundary between us – a strange and cold distance the like of which I had not experienced before. Later, I watched the nightgown wavering, rising from its place and going to stand by the window. She stood right there and said, 'Numan, come to me.' Without being able to tell the difference whether it was an order, a desire, or a plea, I went and stood in front of her. My wife said, 'Look into my eyes, Numan,' in a strange voice and again I could not tell whether it was an order, a desire, or a plea. I looked. Our eyes locked into each other's pupils for a while and our eyelashes waited for the other to waver. She looked deep into my eyes, the way I was lost in hers. This went on till she lowered her eyes and broke contact.

Sakine had two eyes!

When I came to the inn after having breakfast, I kept repeating the same sentence throughout the day:

'Sakine had two eyes!'

Not knowing what was going to happen to me in the evening, I wandered around, anxious like the treasure hunter who finds a treasure under the very house he lived in. I passed a few times by the door of the room of Storyteller Tahir, who told strange stories during the night and remained lost in himself during the day. I walked in and out of the inn's stable. I sat at the place in the hall where this exotic Traveller had sat, the Traveller who had once come to our city and stayed at my inn for two nights. I went and sat near the barbecue, just like Konos, who seeks refuge in my inn on some cold nights to escape from being frozen. I thought of the snoring merchants, the fugitive chieftains, the young married couples who would not give up their desire for each other even in the inn, the travellers who would sleep with their clothes on so that their money was not stolen, and the faded faces who had no other place to go except to the roads. I thought of all these people, each of whom would come at a different time and be the guests at my inn. As you can guess, I did everything necessary to take my wife, Sakine's eyes out of my mind, but to no avail. Because Sakine had two eyes!

But those were such beautiful two eyes that only dream-sellers could sell them. And I thought to myself, how could I have not seen till now those two eyes that greeted me every night, saw me off every morning, looked into my hands, my feet, and even into my eyes? The more I thought, the closer I came to harming myself with my anger.

'Every day you have slept near two bright stars, but you haven't noticed, Numan,' I said to myself. 'You've always had two beautiful countries where no one can go, and still you haven't noticed.' It turned out that I was just like a room of an inn that looked at all its guests with the same eyes. And I was unaware of it. As soon as I thought about this, I felt like curling up and dying. While I was thinking about this, the warning Sakine had given when she was leaving the house and which I had forgotten about due to my disquiet, came to my mind, 'Come early this evening, Numan.' I looked outside, sun was about to set!

If you have never returned to your house as a totally different man one day, you cannot understand how I returned to my house today. Whatever emotions there can be in any man, they are all mixed up inside me. My shame was blocking my excitement; my curiosity and suspicion consumed each other. It was not possible to either put to bed or shelter these heavy guests, who had become guests inside Numan and not in his inn. I entered the house with the weight of an inn that had been relocated with its countless guests. It was in the hands of Sakine, who had become the owner of each of them now, how the inn and the guests would be shown hospitality.

But when I got back home, I could not find Sakine waiting for me, her husband. First, I went to the hall, where embers were still glowing in our red-hot barbecue. I saw a skewer left lying near the barbecue. The barbeque was at its place, where it ought to be always, undisturbed. What worried me was what the skewer, which had left a very thin burning scar on the threads of the carpet due to its heat, was lying there for. Taking care not to let anything bad come to my mind, but with a strange instinct, I went to the kitchen to the place where Sakine had said to me, 'Look into my eyes' in the morning. She was there, in front of the window where I had looked into her eyes. She was there again, waiting for me to look into her eyes. I stood across her and looked. Blood and gore flowed out of my wife, Sakine's eyes, which she had blinded with her own hands and which were still resting on her cheeks.

There are many inexplicable things; the house of words never closes its doors. How should I tell you about this twilight when I came eye-to-eye with Sakine for the second time and about the horror I've fallen into this evening?

I'm Numan.

I am the owner of both this inn and the adjoining house.

Tonight, for the first time, because there's nowhere else to go, I'm no more than a guest at my own inn.

I have been all eyes with Sakine twice today.

Today I understood that I am the owner of the two most beautiful countries of this world and also that I am nothing beside a dark room of an inn.

A single day of blinding of eyes took an immense revenge from me for the years of putting kohl in the eyes.

(The Turkish language phrase 'gözlerine mil çekmek', which has been used in the title of the story, means 'to blind someone with a hot iron'.)

3

THE LAST SHOW OF THE MAGICIAN SEYFETTIN

Talking about the bitter end of Magician Seyfettin, the residents of the Walled City realized that they knew nothing about his life. The story of the life of Seyfettin was a huge gap between the two magic shows – two acts of magic that occupied the stage twice wherein the second time the magic inside the magic fell to the ground with an imposing bright pride. As many remembered, his arrival in the city happened during the great fair that cheered up the lethargic summer days. It's not that they were not amazed to see such a large haircloth tent that was being set up in the old fair square, where melted candies, smells of sweat, fat flies, and passions smiling with difficulty were exhibited, entwined together. While the middle-aged Seyfettin was busy setting up the rain-proof big, black tent that he had made the settlers knit for him, with the help of his two assistants, all eyes were glued on these three strangers. The curious glances tightened the ropes, suspicious questions erected the poles, and the tent was thus made ready for magic events in the middle of the square. The black haircloth tent, set up on four poles and stretched with eight ropes, was waiting like a well which was turned inside out, for the people who would fall into it in a little while.

Bored of the festivities of the fair, which had not changed for years, the people of the city did not delay to gather around this wonder house that was placed in the middle of their lives. They asked Seyfettin's men weird questions to learn about the inside without going in and to solve the magic tricks without knowing the wizard. Seyfettin's men did not see any harm in informing them that the tent they saw was the same tent that was once set up on the banks of the Tigris River in Baghdad and amazed all the chieftains it hosted. They did not forget to add the following immediately:

'It is none other than this tent that put fever blisters on the lips of the Dilber Makbule of Isfahan, whose witchery fascinated everyone. Also, it is the same tent that bewildered the Storyteller Tahir, who later came to your city and settled here. So far we have not witnessed anyone who stepped inside and came out the same. Although Ibnü'l Esir have said such bad words about the aspects of magic, we would like to remind you that the scholar of Kazvin, Lütfullah, is among our most valued guest. All this shows that our tent is not just a house of curiosity.'

Magician Seyfettin knew that all humans were butlers of their own curiosity. He knew that even the placement of this large black tent was in itself a magic. Before the fragmented entrance opened for exhibition, the tent would meddle with the mind of the customers, attract them towards it and by all means captivate their curiosity.

Finally, as soon as one of the assistants opened the entrance and the other started collecting money, an accident-prone crowd swarmed in quickly. In the dim light infiltrating from four small windows, smoke of soft-smelling incense was scattered. The candle-lit stage in the middle was completely empty. Who was going to see what in this make-believe solitary place, away from the world?

Just the way he knew about curiosity, the Magician knew well about its effect along with anticipation. There was this crucial aspect of the wait – while the people in the tent were waiting, the darkness inside made them anxious and they would shrink into themselves with each passing moment. They would lose their strength and confidence and would even look at themselves as if they were looking at strangers. At that very moment, Seyfettin would throw himself on the stage with the loud clanging of a musical instrument, into that space which was detached from the world and was ready for all kinds of deceptions. He would then begin pulling wool over everyone's eyes.

He did the same that day, too. After keeping his audience in their hapless darkness, he came on the stage with a loud noise that dispersed the heavy air of impatience. Two more candlesticks were lit as soon as he arrived on the stage, illuminating the one-man platform entirely.

Two candlesticks were lighted, because light and magic spell were brothers. Nobody doubts the light. Whoever wanted to hide, hid not in darkness but in light actually. And in that brightness, everyone would see the magician before the magic. Now Seyfettin was a dungeon upon which all their attention gathered. He resembled an endearing Ifrit on the stage with his narrow body, a pair of iridescent eyes that could look at everyone at the same time, a very thin moustache, and fingers that kept wiggling without break. Those inside the tent could find nothing to love or hate him. They could not think that this mischievous body that had come into existence by collecting little pieces from different people, even sheltered a man in it. When he pulled out his wand and started his first trick, Seyfettin and the magic of Seyfettin changed places immediately. All eyes were now on the wand, which was constantly breaking into pieces, then reuniting, and fires erupted from whatever it touched.

It was right in the middle of his magic trick that Seyfettin saw two shining eyes among the audience. He saw not curiosity in those eyes but the one who makes one curious; not the one to submit to magic but the one who made one bow to magic. It was as if he saw a completely different game that spoiled his magic – a show inside a show, a magic inside magic.

When those eyes he was glued to swallowed the brightness of the stage that deceived eyes, the Magician's hands started to shake for the first time. He got confused as he went from one magic to another and for the first time, no pigeons came out of the white handkerchief that he waved. He was in trouble. Till now he had made others wonder what he was hiding, whereas now he, the one who made people wonder, had turned into wondering. The strings of the pair of eyes that he did not know what they hid, had remained entangled with his fingers. Except for the eyes that locked into his eyes, no one understood what happened. At that moment the magic ended and the tent folded. Time had long ago made him forget himself and also his unfinished tricks when he made his comeback after many years and performing his last big show.

Who knows, maybe that was what the magician wanted – to be forgotten!

Perhaps, Seyfettin continued to wear himself out to break the spell of that gaze of the pair of eyes that ruptured not only his magic, but the mirror of his fortune as well, on that day when everybody forgot about him.

No one knew what he did in the long void of his life in which he got lost among all the missing things and never set up his tent again. No trace of him was found again in the city, and no rumours were spread about him being on any trail either. He was just an unfinished magic story that appeared and disappeared once in a while, along with his birds, cages, handkerchiefs, swords, and fire-swallowing wand. Like every forgotten person, people forgot him, too.

But one day, when he set up his huge haircloth tent again in the middle of the fair to complete his unfinished magic, the sleeping angel of reminiscence also came to life. With the same summoning voice, the curious people filled the tent. The same pair of eyes went inside and set up at the same place, from where they had earlier spoiled the show. The two candles flared up again and Seyfettin again jumped on the stage with the loud clanging of a musical instrument. Later, no one ever forgot the last show of the Magician.

By setting himself ablaze, he appeared in flames. Everyone initially thought it to be a magic of the Magician. A wheezy sentence poured out of Seyfettin's mouth along with the smell of burnt meat. He howled amid the flames:

'Even the fire does not extinguish the fire.'

4

WISE MANSUR ABANDONS THE CITY

His student had to travel for a long time in the damp, sticky, and shrunk darkness to go to Mansur. It was a terrible summer night. 'Man and the garbage both smell too much,' he said to himself. However, Mansur's student was feeling that the smell was not only the smell of sweat or garbage left on a shore. It was as if an altogether different smell that he could not put a name to had been mixed up. As he walked, he could distinguish this smell from the other smells, but he could not understand where it was filtering from, where it came from, and of what it was. It was a strange smell unlike anything and apparently without any source. It was neither a rotten smell of a corpse that the winds brought from afar nor a burnt smell. It was not the smell of a reed bed and of course not the smell of incense. When Mansur opened the door and called his student inside, the student was still engrossed in the smell that he could not put his finger on. Suddenly, the student wondered why he was called upon there. But he sent the question in his mind back to the place where it came from, to the streets, and then entered the house, passing through the doorstep.

He stepped inside in the same way as he had been doing for thirty years. He passed through the big courtyard as he had been doing for thirty years. He opened the door of the big room, where they had spoken to each other face-to-face tim, again for thirty years, with the same familiarity. He opened the door but upon seeing a thirty-year-package compiled and collected inside, for the first time he did not know what to do in the room. He did not know, because he was disciplined in silence and obeying. He would not question unless he was extended the hook of a question. He would not speak until Wise Mansur untied the knot of the rope of reverence present on his tongue.

However, he was both confused and impatient – all the mattresses were gathered, the quilt was rolled up, the books were tied up in bundles, the ink pot was placed in the bedding roll, and the tip of the pen-case was turned in the direction of the road. The memories trembling in the brightness of the lamp were left behind to be gathered – heartbeats of thirty years, words hanging in the emptiness of the room, lectures delivered. The very long silences stripped off the attire of desire and the clear smiles that took pains to not ruffle even a single silk of it, were left behind. All these belonged to both of them. Wise Mansur did not want to touch any of them without the presence of his student. The student felt himself to be like the snow that was put in a copper bucket and hung over the firewood and thus was melting. He had understood that this call from his teacher was the last call. He was to be given his share of what they had accumulated for thirty years. He had understood this morning that a word will be cut in half right from the middle.

'Thirty years,' said Wise Mansur and started the conversation.

'You have been with me for exactly thirty years and you will no longer be with me from now on. The pen-case that mediated my words will no longer be held in your hands. In the morning, we will split into two hearts that are the same from inside.' Later, without taking a break, he explained the reason that brought the passenger to the road.

'I used to liken the Walled City to a person. I would think of the houses as cells, count the alleys as the thin veins in our bodies, compare our main roads to our thick veins and accept the city square as our heart. Clean blood flowed from all sides to the heart of the Walled City. Her palpitations were precise and healthy, but not anymore. For thirty years now, when I came here and you became my student, I listened to her with the attention of a physician, leaning my ears against her body. I watched the blood, barely flowing into the streets, roads, and insides of houses from its exhausted heart that had lost its excitement. You also know that nothing except death stays between a person and life in a city that is too tired to sin, too cowardly to dare to steal, and forgotten in a manner that it cannot be brought back to memories. It is the thought of death that makes knowledge attractive. People want to know everything about this huge house where they have been guests for a while before death comes and perishes them. It is our duty to lead these curious immigrants to the last door without letting them digress into wrong paths. But the Walled City resembles a depleted pinch of grass on its own grave. That last door was almost the city itself. It is not that there is no one among us who can feel it. A few sensitive souls are preparing a noisy death feast to give life to the life of this abandoned plain land of this world. I see countless lines and countless signs on the faces of those who entered and passed through my doorstep, whose enthusiasm was exhausted with time. Even the accident-prone guide, who we call knowledge, loses its way in a flash. This city exhausted me even more than you can imagine,' said Mansur and continued with his conversation in this manner.

As he spoke, his student felt like drowning in the dark sea that swallowed everything inside it. Finally, Mansur went into the room where he had spent all his youth by retiring into seclusion and began to wait for the morning, laying the ground cloth of silence under him.

And his student also began to wait. It was the last time that he was on duty to keep the vigil on all the words in the hall where the translated treatises of Plato, Brahman teachings, and works of Ibn Bedran, Ibn Ferhun, Rüşd, and Gazali were all bundled up and filled in saddlebags. This night resembled the first night that he came to the Walled City, breaking away from his days full of love with Şehribal, who got a bad name for herself in Balkh. Just like that night, he was all alone, without any base, and abandoned. He had not become attached to this city where he lived, but he was attached to his Master, who lived in this city. What were the countless words in these piles of books he was crouching besides, in the absence of Wise Mansur, who gave life to them, but just a valley of ink that had dried up? For once, untying the strings of decorum, he could have asked his Master to take him along. But

24

once that string is untied, how would it hold the knot as before? He stopped thinking. Under the heavy shadows of the lamp, he listened to the heartbeats of his teacher in the next room. The heart beat and time continued to create waves in the agonizing sea of waiting until morning.

When it was time to leave in the morning, Wise Mansur said to his student:

'Time also has a smell. The smell you felt in the dark yesterday was the smell of time. That smell is felt only when a city starts to sink.'

5

THE HORSE WITH NO MEMORIES RUNS FASTER

When the governor of the Walled City died, the city council gathered in anxiety, believing that an empty throne would only serve the devil. With the responsibility that came with experience, they came to such a decision after measuring and weighing each word that came out of their mouths – let us send a messenger to each of the two sons of the governor in the two distant cities, located on the other side of the mountains with eerie summits, sharp cliffs, and desolate valleys, which could only be reached with very long and narrow roads. Both the messengers should set off when the sun starts to show the colour of the yarn. Let's make him our governor, whose chest is wide, whose horse is fast, and whose sleep is less. The decision pleased all those in the council. The two messengers loved both sons of the governor equally. They descended slowly from the slopes by putting a bridle on time, with food in their saddle bags, and the decision of the council in their breasts.

The two messengers went down the slopes. They rode their horses side-by-side, along the distant plains, without talking to each other. After crossing the soft lands, leaving the prints of horseshoes, both of them reached the foot of the Yunt Mountain, filled with eryngo plants and pebbles. They climbed down from their horses and hugged each other. They said, 'We are carrying a message, split up into two parts, of which one is not more important than the other and also should not reach later than the other. We have to finish the journey we started. On the fourth day, when the sun is fully centred in the sky, let us both take this load off at the same time.' Then the message was split up into two. The two messengers whipped through the two separate skirts of the mountain.

When the messengers reached the sons of the governor to give the bad news and the good news of the throne, they found the younger son resting on the edge of the river and the elder one inspecting the stablemen on the farm. First they announced the bad news. Both sons thought of their father's face – that plain and anguished face, which saw so many sieges, lines of which were tested by so many enemies, and which had to fend off so many betrayals. Like every son, they too felt insecure and a part of them missing, until the messengers gave them good news of the throne. The ambition of power became a boat of fire in the dark sea of pain and began to swim. They sent away the memories of their father, who took care of them since their birth, immediately. They set out for the throne, which passed through the planer of years and therefore demanded attention for its balance. The throne would belong to the one who reached the city first.

The horse of the elder son was cut off from its herd when it was just a small colt and brought to the farm. It had been raised as a racehorse. It did not know what a mother's smell was. It had seen its mornings in a dark stud farm for years. It was trained in the racecourse during the daytime and it did not have any other use than just running fast. When it looked at the mountains beyond the fences, it lacked all the different kinds of memories that would freshen its mind. It ate whatever was put in front of it and lived unaware of all the flavours of nature except the grass on the edges of the farm. The only thing that this horse, with sturdy hooves, thick mane, and strong calves, knew was to run relentlessly when its rider's whip touched its skin. And that is what it did. When its master mounted its back and released its bridle free, there was nothing left behind to think about. It leapt forward from its harness and kept running.

The horse of the younger son had grown up on the slopes of the hills. It had the memories of the warmth of the children caressing its soft hair when it was just a small colt, and also the coolness of the river that left bubbles all over its body when it took a dip. It had the memories of the smell of different kinds of plants on every hill that left flavours totally different from each other in its mouth. It had the memories of the silent sentimentality of the fellow horses of its herd and of course, of the gentle face of its old master, who gave it to the governor as a gift while training it. It was not just a horse, but a beauty of the countryside with its hooves that deserved silver horseshoes, silk-like mane and slender pasterns. Its life was attached to this place, just like that of a waterfront willow. For him, a faraway place was the flat area where the mountain disappeared into the plains. It had felt in its heart that it would forever lose the image of the mountain it grew up on, when the young son rode on its back and released its bridle to reach the throne of the Walled City. It went back and forth between its memories and the desire of the young son. It pretended to be running.

The days that solved the unknown also began to unravel the secret of the new governor at the end of the first warm season, which burned the nails of the birds on the rooftops. When the thickness of his fake eyebrows, the blindness of his blurry eyes, and the words of his bloody tongue turned into laws, the days of prosperity of the people began to come to an end gradually. The city's veins clogged a little more every day. It was overcome by languor and became paralysed. The deadness emanating from the copper buckets that lost their tin, the fountain troughs that held moss, smoke stains of the lamps on the walls, the flies that filled the market place, shadowed time piling upon each other like that of a lace work. The life of the streets was extinguished in such a gradual manner, that no one noticed in the beginning the jamming of this huge system, which was losing blood. When they realized it, even Moneylender Nizamettin, who had faced countless disasters of the city with courage, wished to get out of this shattered city after giving away his third daughter.

The people of the city, trying to comprehend what had struck them, decided to consult the mind of Wise Mansur's student, the hinges of whose door were rusted, for nobody had stepped in for a long time. The only reply Wise Mansur's student gave to all those who complained about their days of disaster was,'The mind of the horse that brought the elder son to the city was devoid of memories.'

6

THE THREE DAUGHTERS OF MONEYLENDER NIZAMETTIN

Moneylender Nizamettin Mervi summed up his seventy years of life, in which he witnessed all the coquetry of fate and witnessed every flaw of time, in one word – gratitude. Gratitude for reaching the present day without breaking the silk thread-like connection between his livelihood and his life in this market place of the Walled City, the city which had been destroyed three times by nature and the ambition for power of the local lords, the city which had been able to stand up on its feet after falling three times on the swings of history. These were the moneylender's last days in this world, standing in front of the door of death, when his joints whined as he straightened up and could not make the sun heal his body. He was now tired after fighting so long with the world, exhausting the world and in turn getting exhausted by it. As he looked at the freckled gold coins he placed on his display window, he said to himself silently, 'I was the one who celebrated the three great destructions of the city with three beautiful festivals.'

Strangely enough, each of those terrible days of life and death that devastated the Walled City caught his wife pregnant, and his wife gave birth to one girl each time while the city tried to mend itself. That is why his first daughter was of the same age as the year of the torrential rains, the second as old as the siege, and the last as the plague. It seemed to Moneylender Nizamettin that the facial features of each of his three daughters were shaped by the painful memories of the time in which they were born. Whenever he looked, he would find the traces of that insatiable storm that

29

he encountered for the first time in his life, in the eyes of his eldest daughter. He thought his daughter had this vein in her that could not be held and dominated by most men. The middle daughter was the work of long, unending siege days, surrounded by enemy lords. She reminded her father of the women exhausted from waiting and the traces of the siege evenings that got embossed on their faces while looking at the mirrors and getting to know themselves again, every single time. With time, Moneylender Nizamettin believed that those who did not pay attention to the beauty of his second daughter's hands – and who did not pay much attention to her thin skin which was always ready to pale, would never make her happy. His youngest daughter looked like a lotus flower hiding in her mother's belly. She was born when the last corpses were being gathered. There was forlornness in her eyes that he could not put a name to. She had no gruffness as was in his eldest daughter, neither had she any curiosity of her other sister. When she looked, it was in a manner that would illuminate even the deepest well she looked into. Moneylender could not unravel the secret of his last child, whom he secretly loved the most. He could not predict what would make her happy.

The adolescence period of his eldest daughter coincided with the time when all of his passions were blinded and began to settle in the countenance inherent in the oriental wisdom. Understanding that it was the time when people would start approaching him and before learning what the people wanting to ask for his girls' hands had to say, Moneylender Nizamettin made his three girls sit near him one evening and said:

'Soon this door will start getting knocked and the reason that brought your mother to me will eventually take you away from me. It is no longer for me, living far away from your age, to find tailors for your fabrics. You chose the next days of your destiny. All I will do is put a key in your hands. I hope you will open the door you are most eager to enter. Ask all your suitors behind that veil this question – 'What did you bring for me?' In this question, your dreams and the imagination of the suitor will be hidden.'

The eldest daughter was very fond of the face of her father. It was a hard-lined face that had just started to get the sheen of wisdom. An intense light used to emanate between his glances, giving a feeling that a flood was ready to burst out. In these facial lines that frightened, terrified, and grilled, then suddenly softened and embraced, there were hints of a safe shelter that would suppress the inherent gruffness and make it acceptable. Every time the large door of the mansion was opened and every time a man sat on the other side of the curtain, she searched only for the signs of this hard and soft father face. It was not at all difficult to understand the words of the speakers behind the curtain as every word has a taste, a tone, and an address. She did not take much time to distinguish that those who used 'river' in their sentences were disloyal and distant, those who promised gardens were soft and feminine, and those who offered palaces were rude and stingy. She heard unheard promises from these strangers sitting on the other side of the veil. She went from city to city, moved from climate to climate, and became a guest from one house to another. Still, she held on to just one sentence from among so many that had been spoken. She decided that only one sentence would not break her trust, 'I brought you a diamond divit (a pen-case with inkwell) with which you can inscribe your name on the rocks.'

The middle daughter's fascination was for her father's profession. Her father knew well the magical relationship between man and woman, which most men could never understand. At times, from his gaze emanated very eager beams of light of a womanizer who had adorned the skins of women with the most beautiful diamonds and then somehow had come to his senses. She loved this look of her father the most among all his looks. She could not help but be envious of the women who were lucky to get these looks in the days of his youth. And she used to say, 'How will a fantasy that was left thirsty by poverty will cover the skin thinned by wealth?' Every time the large door of the mansion was opened for her, every time a suitor sat behind the veil, she sought her father's courtesy that caressed the body more than the soul. She did not face much difficulty in determining that those who used 'rain' in their sentences were gloomy and unbearable, those who talked about 'divit' were logical and cold, and those who offered maids in her service lacked good taste. The middle daughter went on a separate journey with every voice of the face on the other side of the veil. She sat in the palaces near the banks of a river, where the lights of crystal chandeliers fell into the water. She played mother to the countless pet animals on a farm surrounded by forests. She understood how the bales of silk are balanced while loading the silk caravans. She watched the sweating crowd through the windows overlooking a city square. She thought for a long time at each stop she was taken to, but could not find the answer she was looking for until the fortieth suitor knocked on the door. The enthusiasm of the middle daughter had started to decline but this sentence of the fortieth suitor brought it back in place, 'I have brought a turquoise stone washed in my tears for you that will match with the freckles on your neck.'

The youngest daughter was passionate about her father's heart. She knew that he had a heart that would beat differently in each season but also knew how to stay the same at all times. That is why her father was considerate and wise. That is why he was soft against the hard, close against the distant, and supportive to the lonely. He would never walk on the path of prejudice, without the truth of the matter opening up to him. When the large door started to get knocked for her, the youngest daughter sat behind the veil without any expectations. In this state, she looked like the naive birds that took to the roads to reach Simurg, the Magical Bird. She believed those waiting on the other side of the veil would tell her what she had been looking for. This sitting took so long, so long that the whole city started talking about it. Curiosity increased the number of suitors, suitors increased the sentences. Each sentence lighted up a piece of the crystal of truth that existed in her, but somehow she could not find one single sentence that would combine all those pieces together.

Days and months passed by. The youngest daughter learned the different states and aspects of life, death, time, and seasons. She roamed around in the streets of cities she had never been. She got to know the dampness and dinginess of the streets she had never visited. She learnt the names of countless birds, countless fish, countless rivers, and countless mountains. She smelt the flowers that she had never come across. She confronted virtue rolling down the edge of lust and she felt the impatience of lust hidden behind virtue. She had no difficulty distinguishing that some words came from the heart and others only from the tongue.

She mixed up and twisted together all the promises made to her. She passed them through the counter of her mind, filtered, and examined them. She could not decide which colour called out for her on that big dream counter that was revealed in front of her eyes. There were so many people, the world was so big, and life was a mystery.

Moneylender Nizamettin Mervi had almost forgotten the word 'gratitude' that remained on his tongue throughout his life. He was the most impatient among those waiting. It was as if he had never lived, had not seen anything, had not heard anything, and he would only know everything there was to know when he heard the words that would unlock the heart of his youngest daughter. On a summer afternoon, when the sun stretched the shadows of the minarets of the big mosque in the city square, news on the grapevine through the narrow stone streets reached the market place quickly. It reached and untangled Moneylender Nizamettin's tongue that longed to utter the words 'Thank God!'

It was not a sentence but just a silence to which his youngest daughter, whose elegance was reminiscent of the folds of lilac, surrendered herself. No one could understand what she found in the silence of a man who fled from the people and descended into the wells of the night.

7

WHAT HÜSREV TOLD
ABOUT HIMSELF

When I touched the depths of darkness, where I left myself in desperation, a drop of light fell onto me.

This happened when I reached the third step of my thirtieth birthday.

My name is Hüsrev.

My story is simple.

I came to this world on a quiet plain at the foot of one of the distant slopes of the hill, where new flowers bloomed for each newborn of the Walled City. Like any other baby, I too do not remember the moment when I first said 'mother'. But what secretly hurts me is that my mother, tired from the business of the world, also did not remember that moment. I could not tell anyone about the wound caused in a child by the forgetfulness of a mother. This is why I have always been looking for myself in a place far from myself. I later connected this to the reason why, among my friends, I was just like a kite which floated from one hill to another, since its thread had been cut. When I sit today and remember those vast skies, I can grasp better the solitude that grew inside me with age. Houses depressed me, games bored me, and those girls with slender waists who never left their mothers' side, annoyed me. I used to be bored throughout the unending days. I would be sorry not to have wings whenever I saw a bird flying alone in the endless summer afternoons. This must be reason for my passion for horses and love for my mother's distant relative, Stableman Behram – to be able to go away.

Just as my mother did not remember the first time I called her 'mother', I do not remember the moment I entered the Walled City. Maybe this is fate. What I remember is staring at the walls, lit by a flickering, sooty lamp, with dull eyes for whole nights in one of the small rooms of the thick stone-walled school. I searched for myself under the sooty dome for a few years. I, who cursed even the endless borders of plains, was squeezed inside the four walls of the room like a prisoner. A tiring battle, similar to that of adversaries who could not beat each other, continued for a few years between my mind and my heart. I was so tired that I could not even feel the anguish of my heart being defeated. Eventually, I rebelled against my thin neck falling into the book rest and the surrender that the letters wanted from me. When I was sent out of home, while my desire to taste the world with all its brutality remained intact, my heart tried to protect me with mercy and stayed stuck to the stone walls like an ownerless shadow. When I thought about it later, I shuddered when I remembered that I did not worry much about it. Those who spend their lives only in the games of the mind and return to their hearts again one day by a miracle, will understand why I shuddered. Another thing that they will learn is that what is tasted with the mind is always a little bitter and prone to sin. This was taught to me by the Walled City's streets, from even the corners of which many people did not pass.

I cannot speak about what I learnt in the other streets of the city for many reasons, just like no one speaks about how they were once touched and turned into a house of their hearts. The heart does not like remembering the bad, old times that were wasted by the mind. The only thing I will do is give you a few hints that the heart would allow. When a man trusts only his mind, he first pollutes the water and then makes himself believe in the clarity of the same. Whatever he drips into that dirty water, he approves of it all with humane legitimacy. When I was summoned again by my heart one day, I took a last look at the waters polluted by the lonely mind. I looked at them for the last time and I saw ten years of waves crashing into one another. In the journey that I had started as one Hüsrev, countless faces of mine appeared before my eyes, and I could not differentiate which Hüsrev was the real one. Let me explain briefly.

My soul, which I fed with small sins in the beginning, craved for a new evil after every sin it tasted. I wanted evil. In order to suppress the pain that each of my previous mistakes left inside me, I committed an even bigger mistake than the earlier one, every time. After a while, I completely lost control and the clues that I needed to be able to return. Honourable people of the city often do not know that when the shutters go down in the evening, the shutters of another life beyond their imagination are opened. They are unaware that some inns, some rooms, and some corridors are heated only by the steam coming out of the tuberculosis mouths. As I was afraid to bring my eyelids, which had turned black and blue by lust and marijuana, to the sun, I handed myself over completely to that steam of the tuberculosis mouths. For years, I slept in the beds where smoke, sweat, vomit, and eczema got mingled with one another. I took refuge in the warmth of women, none of whom I knew at all. And I was careful to not remain sober enough to even think about the reasons that led men to this entire catastrophe. Hüsrev was falling apart every day, like a tattered rag. I was not in a position to know which part of me was thrown away in which direction. Except for death, I climbed all the steps of the marijuana ladder. I had no wish other than death to be my last visitor in the house of misery. Of course, this is not all that I wanted to say. But my time is limited. Let those who will return to their hearts complete whatever I could say in this limited time.

I am Hüsrev.

On the third step of my thirty years of age, a drop of light fell on me at a moment when my mind had taken me and touched upon the depth of darkness. Just like the way I was born in the plains, I woke up with birds again. Like the alarm of the child who doesn't understand what has happened to him, I showed the dark circles under my eyes and the contemptible scars on my body to the sun. Then I woke up from my sleep and followed the people who called, to their homes. I went and opened a large door and sat behind a thick curtain. She asked me the same question, not a bit more, not a bit less, as she had asked me in my dream:

'What did you bring me?' I did the same what I did in my dream – I remained silent.

36

That day, my unattended heart, which I had left on the stone walls, suddenly came to me and made me listen to its palpitations, as if it was just waiting for the day when the light would fall upon me. Let the rest of the story stay with me; it is both intimate and difficult to tell.

I am Hüsrev.

I understood that there is a bird's breath that blows into the hearts of those who remain away from their hearts and puts them back inside us. I wish that for centuries after me, someone should tell this ordinary story of mine by feeling just like me. He should tell that till the time the core of a person doesn't turn dark, there is always a miracle waiting for every life.

8

THE YOUNG APPRENTICE OF STABLEMAN BEHRAM

The biggest stud farm in the Walled City belonged obviously to the governor. In a huge farm surrounded by solid fences, about a dozen of stablemen were tasked with keeping the horses ready at all times for ostentatious ceremonies, wars awaiting little excuse, and proud excursions of the governor and his guards. The old grooms were experts enough to recognize a horse from the footprints it left on the ground. They knew on their fingertips which horse needed to be whipped on its rump and which horse could be disciplined just by a simple caress to its mane. And they all knew this too that horses, just like humans, got tired one day. Their hooves, too shattered to wear a new horseshoe, their shed teeth and their strangely saddened eyes, separated them from their proud master, whom they carried till then, and their bright medals. They were replaced by wild foals, sometimes born on the farm, often caught and brought from the mountains. The horses recruited from the wandering herds of the high hills were shared among the stablemen and all of them were tamed. Even the most stubborn ones succumbed to the order of the stud farm in a week's time, and bowed to their determined trainers. What happened to Stableman Behram's young apprentice was just a misfortune.

None of you should look down upon his ignorance. He thought that the spirit of this thin, feeble foal was as weak as its calves. And again, he thought, 'Before it gets dark, I must groom this unattractive animal and thus I will get in my Master's good books.' The animal's appearance had misled him, and he had not event thought of turning back to look at his Master while walking towards the foal he chose. Because in such moments, everything can be understood by looking at the master's face. Had he looked back, he would have found two cues present on his Master's whip-skin like hardened face – a sceptical pair of eyes and a sarcastic pair of lips. In other words, a huge question mark full of doubts, which got separated from its apprentice right in the beginning. Nevertheless, the Master did not interfere with his choice. He left his apprentice with his luck when the horses from the wild herd were being shared for training.

At the end of the third day, except for master Behram's apprentice, all the stablemen had put the halters of training on their horses, trained their mouths for bridle, and killed their pride that they had brought with them from the mountains. Once that pride was killed, the horse could be at the command of the governor. The secrets and the skills of grooming a horse were hidden here. Disciplining a horse was a battle of willpower for few days between the knowledge of the stableman and the pride of the horse. Ultimately, the horse would be defeated by the knowledge and the tricks gained from the countless trainings in the stud farm. A good-tempered, graceful, and well-bred animal would take all these virtues from the new impression that life had embedded in the place of its dead pride. There were three impressions that training gave them – compliance, strength, and speed. The other two would be useless without the presence of the first. But the other two were like spouses to each other. If one stumbled, the other also stumbled in trying to follow it. The foals that allowed themselves to be trained properly were released on the slopes of the hills they had come from, once the strength in their calves and the agility of their hooves ended, alongside many other horses, on the slopes that bore the signs of familiarity with human beings.

By the end of the third day, the pride of all the foals was killed and the impression of life was embedded with the groomer's whip in the gap opened in all the foals where their pride resided. But Behram's apprentice had lost his head in such a manner that he could have put the bridle through his own teeth. It was as if this was not a horse in his hand, but a completely different animal that had been carefully raised to avenge all the other horses that had been groomed till date, as if it wanted the revenge for all those horses from whose memories the mountains had been wiped out forcefully, and for all those days in the mountains when they roamed free. Those few days of desperation gave way to this thought of the apprentice and transformed into an obsession. The secret battle of pride he had entered got his nerves on edge and made him furious. He put the rein of all his senses under the order of the whip that he held in his hands. After the third day, his sleep abandoned him and left him in the torments of the darkness of the night along with the blood of the animal he whipped. The whip, which opened big wounds on the skin of the foal, was not able to break the spirit of the animal. On the contrary, it was Behram's apprentice who got wounded in his soul. As the will of his enemy became sturdier with each whip, his own will weakened more and more. His pride died and in fact, it seemed that the horse would practically turn into his groomer.

The obstinacy between the apprentice and the foal lasted seven days. His Master, who had the experience of countless proud horses, watched them carefully for those seven days. The young apprentice was peeved, desperate, and clueless. He was humiliated not only in front of his Master but also in front of his friends. Stableman Behram saw the aimless violence, blindness, and loss of pride, which was embedded in him too by the foals he had once succumbed to, in his apprentice's eyes. The days had grown long. The apprentice lost the difference between the day and night, and the mainspring of his mind had popped up. The showdown between the horse and the apprentice had come to a point of no return. In this green field that everyone thought to be just a farm, a man and an animal can provoke each other to the end. The foal would become irritable every time it saw the apprentice and the apprentice would see only the foal every time he closed his eyes. And finally, it would come to that familiar end.

After losing his beloved Mahinur to the Traveller Battuta, Stableman Behram, who gave all his life to the profession of his ancestors in the steppe, and who knew how to take the nastiness out of the stubborn foals as one unearths a treasure carefully. At the end of the seventh day, Stableman Behram sat between the horse and the apprentice with a dead body and his almost dead pride, respectively. And he said to him:

There are three kinds of horses that come from the herd. Some horses quit their nastiness just by hearing the sound of the whip being hit on the other horses; there is no distance between their souls and their skins. Some horses come and go between their spirits and their wounds caused by the whip. As the wounds get bigger, the distance between their souls and their skins closes eventually. When blood drops into their spirits, they surrender themselves.

Then there are some horses, the distance between whose spirits and their bodies gets bigger with each stroke of the whip. The more you whip it, the more it will become impossible to catch its spirit. Only a lifeless body of a foal remains in the end. And among them, there is one which remains in the memory of the groomer, whose pride could not be broken and who broke the pride of the groomer. Mastery does not lie in taming these foals; rather it lies in not touching them at all. The whip is just an excuse for those who are willing to come to the path.

9

WHEN THE TRAVELLER LEFT

ALIF

Mahinur looked at the garden shadowed by the chestnut tree from the edge of the window. She watched the drooping shoulders of the Traveller, who was walking towards the garden gate. She watched his dragging feet and his dispirited neck that would not turn back. Already, a bond that would never break and a distance that would never be covered had occurred between the one bidding farewell and the one bidden farewell. She remembered the moment when she had first seen him. She had run to the mirror. She had discovered with fear and astonishment how the spark inside her changed the Mahinur on her face. Then she had tried to drive this riddle away from her solitary mind by hiding behind her veil. Now, she was wondering not about the reunited but the separated Mahinur's face. But she could not dare to see this second face despite wanting to so much, just like the Traveller, who could not look back while going away. She knew that this second face would shatter the former in the mirror and leave a severe fracture that would never be cured. While the garden gate was closed for the last time by a man, whose soul had been stolen by the roads, she felt like a very long and thin line, standing at the beginning and not uniting with any other letter.

VAV

From the edge of the window, Mahinur looked at the garden where the Traveller had left his shadows. The owner of the shadows must have reached the city square at this moment. Of course, she knew the roads leading to the city square but for the

42

first time, she realized with surprise that she never knew where those roads were going. 'Where does a road go?' she asked herself, 'where does a road go?'

A person discovers the obscurity of the roads only when they send off a traveller without an address. The one who went, travelled just one road; the one who stayed, remained doomed to unravel the mysterious knots of the countless roads. One could never know whether the person who left, went on the road of death, or the road of betrayal, or the road of reunion. The one who bid farewell got divided into many journeys with the one whom they bid farewell. Many roads passing through different mountains, reaching many different cities, staying in different inns and perhaps finding solace in many different women. As Mahinur thought of the roads, she felt that the Traveller drew a curve upon the thin and long line that did not unite with any other letter and around those eyes while he left the door and trailed off to faraway places. The line now looked like a black braid of hair where the countless roads with no destinations crisscrossed – a thick luxuriant braid inside of which only a single hair belonged to her.

JEEM

Mahinur's eyes moved from the garden to the naked mountain on the border of the city. This was no longer the same mountain that she had been looking at since the day she was born. As she looked at its bare body that had lost all its adornment, she understood that she herself and the city also migrated along with the Traveller to the countless unknown places through the countless roads. That inn that hosted the Traveller for the first time in the city, that run-down square, those secluded neighbourhoods – what were these but a heavy memory that left the shadows of the two eyes which gave life to them? So far, many acquaintances had gone, but the city always stayed here with its own colour and smell. However, now what stood between this stark-naked mountain and the completely alone Mahinur was not a city but a confused, impoverished, and dateless vacuum. Vacuum! Mahinur finally removed that vacuum and became a part of the imposing mountain. She got acquainted with the brutal peak of being alone there. She saw the terrible loneliness of self-confidence. The

43

heaviness of being abandoned grew so big on her shoulders that for a moment she wished to get rid of that burden forever. But the Almighty, who burdens humans and unburdens them and whose mercy is abundant, took a pity on Mahinur. The curved line, starting from the eyeballs and going far away, gathered in the shape of a half-moon and came back to her. A dot of the half-moon appeared in her stomach, an indescribable twitch. At that moment, Mahinur rushed to the mirror again. She saw the puzzled, hopeful, and bruised traces of a new body, added to her body, on her face.

LAMALIF

Mahinur did not go near the window again that day. She kept away from the shadows that the Traveller had left in the garden, the city that was without the Traveller, and the uncovered mountain that would almost swallow her. She sat in a corner and opened the bundle of her fidgety memories and began to arrange them in a way that she would never forget them. She thought about the Traveller being the guest of her father, Miniaturist Burhanettin. She thought about the first time she saw his face first through the corner of a window, then through a gap in the door and then through the open door. She thought about the strong friendship between the two men. She thought about the days when all three got tied together by a silk thread-like bond. But whatever she thought, she returned to that first moment, that afternoon when she looked into the eyes of the Traveller. When she first looked into them, she had seen countless roads in his eyes. She had thought that he would put a knot on all the other roads and keep open only the path that came to her. However, later she had not been able to do anything except watching his face with fear that gathered a little more dust from the roads he had not been able to take. His face turned into a house of suffering, slowly, because of not being able to take the roads. Finally, while thinking about that gentle face that could be polished by the cities, she confessed in desperation – time just blocked the road between the two of us.

HOUSEKEEPER

I am Mahinur. I am the daughter of Miniaturist Burhanettin and the wife for two years of the Traveller from Tangier, and then abandoned by him. I lived like a precious gift for two years, between the two men, of which one had the traces of all the miniatures in his face and the other had the signs of all the roads that could not be taken, in his face. They looked at my face gently, listened to my words with attention, and laughed childishly at my inexperience. A golden ribbon wrapped all the sides of my life; I am grateful for it. I was sixteen years old, now I am twenty-six. Even for once I did not think about cutting the strings of attachment with the scissors of rebellion. I also did not consider replacing the fate God has assigned to me with another that God would not have minded if I did. It was as fast as the way I matured in the company of the Traveller, to enlarge the reward inside me of my two joyful years, the like of which I knew I would never experience again. Especially my father's disappearance after he did the last miniature brought us even closer to each other.

I am Mahinur. I became the daughter of one and the wife of the other, of the two men who always lived their lives feeling this incompleteness inside them and whose lives got caught in miniatures and the roads. Both of them were too little to be angry with and too big to be forgiven.

10

THE LAST MINIATURE OF THE MINIATURIST BURHANETTIN

Miniaturist Burhanettin, now in the miniature workshop where he worked as the chief miniaturist, was sitting cross-legged in the dimly-lit courtyard and thinking about the twelve long years he spent with his master from the city of Merv.

'Twelve long years surrendered to the intrigues of the soul in an abyss where only lines and colour elves could enter,' he thought to himself. For all these years, which gave him everything he owned and took everything he possessed, he had been a dream apprentice who went back and forth between the eyes and the hands of his master. He paid attention to the eyes when he felt unbearable loneliness and to the hands when his heart overflowed with love.

Burhanettin looked into the two eyes of his master because they had a certain kind of a charm that reduced his agony with their light. This charm attached the apprentice truly to his master. He looked at the two hands because these hands provoked Burhanettin to grasp and then distil anything and everything that overflowed from his heart into the colours. The seasons passed in this manner. He could no longer tell to which month or which year the light filtering through the dome of the miniature workshop belonged. But one day, his master decided to leave Burhanettin alone with Burhanettin's colours. At the end of the twelve years for which his body almost forgot to sweat for the world, the door of the miniature workshop opened and Burhanettin was handed

46

over to the fate of his own colours and lines. When the door of the miniature workshop opened, his master untied the rope with which he had wrapped Burhanettin and his eyes, and sent him off to the city from where he had come, without uttering a single word.

The way back turned into an agonizing distance of uncorrelated questions added end-to-end for the miniaturist, who knew that he was shown the door ahead of time. He sealed the hills he wandered on with a question mark and the waters he passed over with another question mark. When he took a break, he tried to find out the reason for his being sent off, recollecting step-by-step the system of the miniature workshop once again in his mind. His finishing of papers was flawless. No one was better than him in stretching out muraqqa, crushing gold, or making brush. His master preferred him to prepare his paints and wanted him to look into the matter of the consistency of ink. Most importantly, his master liked the miniatures he made and after inspecting them, mostly gave him a warm look. Burhanettin became suspicious when he thought about his master smiling at him. And this suspicion remained with him till he reached the Walled City. He recalled all the smiles his master gave him until he arrived in the Walled City. He came across those two eyes repeatedly. He measured and weighed them, then tried to come to a decision. He saw in the face of his master, which he looked into by dividing it into countless pieces, the hidden hint of some missing lines he had left in his miniatures. His was not only affirming, but also cautioning the smile. When he entered through the gates of his city, he found the reason for which he had to leave his master's house. But he fell into the dungeon of a much more burning question:

'What was missing in my miniatures?'

Not only while entering the city, but also when he entered this building where he was made the chief miniaturist, Burhanettin had the same question in his mind. He spent twelve years alongside his master, almost as many years alongside the question that his master made him ask himself. Just like now, sitting under the dome, from the little holes of which light filtered through, he repeatedly thought about what that missing line was. He thought and realized that it was a line that could not have been found by thinking. He thought to himself that now, when the question and the one who caused that question got intermixed, it was time to return to the doorstep he was thrown out along with the question. He would go to the house of his friend and get warmed up once more in that lamp. Without tearing the curtain of decency, he would expect him to imply the missing line again.

However, a wish inside a wish appeared inside Burhanettin. If he was going to visit his master, wasn't it necessary to paint the most beautiful miniature that would open his heart? Burhanettin kept looking at the manila paper for days without knowing what to paint for his master. For many days, neither a red fire burned nor a star appeared in the blue cloth. He waited for days for his memory to bleed and his spirit to fluctuate. The question, which had been on his mind for years now, infiltrated into his heart unnoticed and left a desert with extinguished torches. The chief miniaturist looked at that desert in agony and wandered in it for the first time with such a rebellion. Although he knew that in the desert of rebellion, if a man waited for another fire, he could not get himself away from it. Until one night, when he saw that from the colours in front of him, red had started to burn. That night he surrendered his hands to the flames of this sudden glowing fire. He took his mind away from his hands, along with his heart and left them alone with each other.

Miniaturist Burhanettin was unable to grasp what he was painting that night, the boundaries of which were ambiguous. When the time turned into a wavy lake, his mind fell into it like a pebble, only to get lost. It seemed as if another miniaturist, who had been hidden inside him for years, came out, solved the longings that he could not solve for years alongside his master, and began to avenge for the miniatures he could not make in front of him. Seasons were bursting out of Burhanettin, sighs stuck in his chest, the desires of adolescence sacrificed in a dimly-lit miniature workshop and the dreamy glances. Burhanettin was watching with surprise his own self as a second miniaturist who had escaped from his chest. He felt with surprise that his body was getting lighter and losing its stiffness. It was getting mixed with colour and taking a new shape inside them. His hands and heart continued on their way by adding time to the colours with an improvisation that he could not understand. When the road finally ended, so did Burhanettin. When the first light of the day infiltrated from the dome of the miniature workshop and touched the miniature he had made, the chief miniaturist could not bear the revenge that the other miniaturist inside him had taken and collapsed right there.

Burhanettin, the chief miniaturist of the Walled City, was all alone when he set out for Merv to see his master. He took neither the picture he made nor the other miniaturist inside him. The secret that had tied him to himself for years had mingled in countless colours and revealed itself to him. He had understood that his master had watched the other miniaturist inside him for those twelve years he spent in the dimly-lit courtyard of the miniature workshop. His master had understood that his apprentice would never go out opening the door of reverence and threw him out of his door lest the knot accumulating inside him got the best of him. The door had opened so that he should not harm the other miniaturist he had imprisoned inside him. His master had seen what he had hidden inside him, understood that he was leaving something incomplete in every miniature he did, and that is why he had given the silk-thread belt in his own hands. His master never touched the pain inside Burhanettin, but had played countless games with him without him realizing it so that the fine blood-river should not drown his apprentice. When he thought about it, Burhanettin couldn't hold the tears in his eyes. While exiting the gate of the city, he mumbled under his breath, filled with over-fatigue:

'My master knew the miniature I was going to do from the beginning.'

49

11

KONOS, THE BANDIT

In the days when even the falling of a leaf was enough to disturb the peace of mind of the people, the blood of an ill-sorted person, who was given the name Konos, began to flow through the veins of the city. He came at times to wake them up in the grouchy mornings that did not want to wake up. He occasionally added an unexpected turmoil to their sluggish afternoons. Some evenings, he enjoyed the change of guard with the setting sun and many nights he gave a gift of horror to the people that roughed up their breaths.

Konos came to visit the city, where he was born and raised for twenty-two years, as a bandit. He came and took foals from the stables, gold from the trunks, clothes from the closets, and put his fear in their place. Then he returned to the mountains. He intercepted the travellers and troubled them. He sent messages to inform that in exchange for their lives he wanted hot bread, fresh meat, and clean clothes. Nevertheless, he did not smear two stains on his pleasure of humiliating others – he never attempted to taint anyone's honour and he did not smudge his sword unnecessarily. The people of the Walled City eventually honoured all the stealing and causing trouble of this clumsy and ugly bully who came out from among them with a common name – the horse thief.

While he was alive, people saw three faces of the horse thief Konos that veiled each other and made them forget about the other two. These three faces were of his childhood, his banditry, and his sainthood. The first face was given to him by his mother, the second by the mountains and the tortures, and the third by the fountain with the image of the moon in it. He was innocent and ugly at first. Then he became innocent, ugly, and scary. And finally, he became innocent and ashamed. Konos fastidiously kept vigil on all the three faces and he could not remain comfortable without showing all his three faces to the mirror of the Walled City.

As a child, he was a cursed, mischievous youngster who spoilt games, broke window panes, scuffled with dogs, and swore curses in the city square that was burdened by the years. He spent almost every moment he breathed in disrupting the comfort of others. It was as if those still, dead, fainthearted neighbourhoods would be buried in silence for eternity if he did not start up a quarrel. Undoubtedly, it was believed that this ugly and unbearable buffoon would eventually come around. He would grow with time, get pushed to the wall by the dregs of adolescence, and eventually surrender to the softness of a bed and the boundaries put by a woman full of trickery. However, it did not happen so. The day he left his childhood, Konos abandoned his childhood face and the city as well.

This happened one morning at dawn. Initially, his intention was to go to distant places which would not send him back. When he started to climb the first slope just outside the city, his emotions withheld the courage to fulfil his intention from him. He turned and looked at the Walled City – this old city, which stood in front of him with its streets suffering from desolation, trees with fruits rotting on their branches, the gardens squeaking their doors, and the lace pillows, the whites of which caused agony, once again made Konos' hatred rise again – his hatred and his passion. It was at this moment that he decided, for the first time, to stay in the mountains. That day, for the first time, he went down to show his devotion and his villainy. He took the chestnut horse, harbinger of the spoils that he would collect for twenty-two years, from the stable that night, for the first time. This second face, which started its time when he stole his friend horseshoer Fettan's horse, became the mirror of fear of the city later.

Despite the fineness of his plans and all his agility, there definitely were times when the traps came out to be more cunning than him. Konos got caught because of the guards of the governor and sometimes because of the caution of the owners of the goods.

First they warned him, then they scolded him, then they beat him, and finally they tortured him in such a way that his face became even uglier. After every torture, the face of the horse thief took another form. The flesh taken out by the pincers gave way to scars that would frighten people. But somehow he got out of prison every time and returned to the mountains. And he did not refrain from making them pay even more every time for what was done to him. The city and Konos were playing a strange game with each other that could show their mutual fidelity only by treating the other badly.

When the horse thief took a break from his job and got lost, people started to secretly wonder about him. Many times it happened that they waited for Konos in a manner one waits for their son, forgetting the horses he stole, the gold he put in his pocket, the clothes that he took which they had got carefully stitched at the tailor shop, and the fear that they felt when he suddenly came out in front of them on the roads. While waiting, some of them silently looked over the mountains and some women even secretly prayed for him. People who went down to the market place hoped to get the news of stealing of horses from the stable of an inn. But they got no such news.

It seemed that if Konos died or got lost, his absence would clog the breathing tube of the city and the whole city would be unable to breathe. When the city waited for Konos, he would be a guest of the neighbouring cities for a while, either to sell what he had stolen, or to get treatment for some disease he suffered from, or to protect himself from the cold of the mountains in the winter. He stayed in inns, talked to people, became friends with someone using the small crumbs of amiability that were still in him, and he would praise his city to his new friend. Konos would tell them about the Walled City where he was born and raised. He would do this with an inexhaustible passion. Sometimes he would even look for a friend so that he could praise his city. He could not sleep in the rooms of those inns for many days and thought about the Walled City for hours. After a period of separation, he would return to the mountains to flex the veins that filled with yearning, and waited like distressed lovers for the time when it would get dark. The city, that woke up cursing Konos, and Konos, who felt intoxicated by being able to scare the city once again, would both take a breath of relief the next morning. By the twenty-second year of banditry, the city and Konos were two lovers who could not share the same house but could not live without each other either.

In the twenty-second year of banditry, Konos came down to the city for the last time without knowing that it was his last time. At midnight, under a cursed rain, he was trying to reach the city square as quickly as possible. He heard that the good-hearted Muhyettin was to be hanged that night. He sensed that if they killed him, something would go amiss inside his own self that he could not put a name to. He decided to save the prisoner if he could. However, the road constantly withheld Konos. He pushed his horse into a swamp and dragged his whip for a long time along the river to find a wide and shallow place to get out. When he reached the city, Muhyettin's account book in the world had already been closed. He watched the very thin dead man under the rain. He looked at him with despair for a long time. And for the first time, he felt as if he was in a foreign city. He came out of the sunshade under which he was hiding himself and returned quickly to the mountains.

During those three days when the rain mercilessly poured down, sitting inside his shelter, Konos thought about Muhyettin, who was hanged in the square and about what happened to those who were hanged. On the night of the third day, when the clouds left the sky, he threw himself out of his shelter. He came down to a water body nearby. He bent down and touched his lips to the water with the reflection of the moon in it. He touched it and whatever happened, happened at that moment. He saw that all his scars and ugly lines abandoned his face one by one and flowed into the water, filtering through the canals along the contours of the very lonely Walled City. As he looked into the water he saw that features of a different Konos were getting shaped in his face. This became the last face of Konos – enlightened and embarrassed.

Enlightened and embarrassed Konos knew that he no longer had any accounts to settle with the Walled City. That secret bond, that passion and hate bond that connected him to the city, which even he could not give a name to, had come apart. He left the shelters in which he hid, the shadows under which he cooled down, and the pathways he tread upon for years and returned to the city. He settled in a half-derelict house on a slope where the borders of the city ended and the borders of the mountain began. The people of the Walled City were unable to unravel the secret hidden in the return of this tired body, which had excited the city for years.

The silence of Konos, who never went out of his house and did not speak to anyone, gave birth to a new kind of fear in the evenings of the city. In the evenings, those who passed the road along the derelict house of Konos, tried to get away immediately. They said that strange noises came from inside the house and they saw many faces of different shapes around it. However, Horseshoer Fettan, who came to the house of Konos drenched in perspiration, found him dead in that somewhat dark room illuminated by a lamp. The next day they buried him right where he died.

Even after his death, Enlightened Konos continued to heal the city's wounds with Fettan, the caretaker of his tomb.

12

MUHYETTIN'S DRY SHIRT IN THE RAIN

It was the twenty-third day of the Dhu'l-Hijja (the twelfth
month of the Islamic calendar) when Hangman Mikdat put the
oiled noose around Muhyettin's neck. As was the tradition, the
execution was carried out at mid-night in the city square. That
night it rained as it had never rained before. The head jailor,
two attending court clerks, and eight guards, who were ready to
carry out the execution orders of the state, were eagerly waiting
for everything to finish quickly. The dark clouds which opened
their shutters and poured water into the city, slowed down the
time and triggered the feeling in twelve of the thirteen individuals
present – except for Muhyettin, who would soon be hanged – that
they would never be able to return home ever again. Also, this
death, accompanied by the rain, aroused misgivings in them. How
relaxed they would be once they got rid of this body, whose end
had come and was delivered into their hands. Finally, Hangman
Mikdat gave life into the night of death by moving the stool from
its place amid a lightning bolt, a few dog barks, and the sounds
of the rain.

Rain flowed over Muhyettin's body until morning. First of
all, Mikdat compassionately tried to soften the neck, on which
the rope was tightly fitted, and the swollen veins. He touched the
stiffened fingers and tried to support the feet that were cut off
from the ground. As it convulsed, he soaked the body with water,
adding coolness to the burning blood in the torso.

55

Later, Muhyettin died. His was a very slender death seen off by the incessant rain. When Muhyettin died, a wound that no one saw but which was to remain for ever, opened in the Walled City square. When the gloominess that his death caused the city was forgotten, the master craftsmen would pass by, stepping on that wound and go to their jobs. The kids would run over that wound, the women would gossip there, Hangman Mikdat, who was like a display window of the last breaths, would wander around the place where he had pulled the stool, just like the way he did in the case of other deaths, to believe that there was no trace left on his hands, which had a touch of criminality. Muhyettin was going to be held at the city square for three days to set an example. Like the other hanged men, he would also leave as much gloom as his death could leave on the souls, but his place in the memories would disappear with his body. The only thing that distinguished Muhyettin from the rest was the rain that never ended.

Those who were hanged were kept suspended by the rope for three days in the square of the Walled City for setting an example. The gallows, which were left in the square for three days as a proof of the power of the governor who punished wrongdoing, and which also showed the helplessness of the people, were lifted and taken away silently at the end of the third day. At such times, a pall of gloom spread over the city. Time would open and close like a crestfallen curtain and restlessness would fall upon not only the people but even the animals. The power of death would knock down the courage of life, and those who would try to go to sleep would be tossing and turning in their beds as they had nowhere to retreat. It would be difficult to come to terms with death for everyone who came down to the square in the daytime. They would approach the gallows with mercy, pity, and prayer; with hate and throaty spittle; with fear and a trembling soul; with indifference and empty eyes – because the windows to look at death are different just the way they are different to look at life. But this death was still a difficult reckoning to come to terms with for most of the people of Walled City. The square grew, grew, and grew, turned into a huge abyss, invisible ropes got wrapped around the necks of people and even if for a moment, everyone got a taste of their own judgement day.

The accounts of fear, hate, or mercy did not matter in the case of Muhyettin's corpse. For this peculiarity, everyone came down to the square full of curiosity, the sorrowful leaving their sorrows behind, the vengeful leaving their vengeance behind, and the coward leaving their cowardice behind. The oddity of this time did not resemble any of the past eccentricities that had made an impression in the memory of the Walled City. The rain that started on the night when Muhyettin was pulled on the rope continued for two more days at short intervals, the sky did not open even once, and the sun was not born. Even the ceilings of the houses started to become damp because of this heavy rain. The strange thing was this – in those short intervals when the rain stopped before it started again, one part of Muhyettin's clothing right on the top of his chest, the size of a palm, was becoming dry in a flash. First a woman saw this, then a madman, and then a guard. People filling the square would wait for the rain to stop and when it did, they stared at the top of Muhyettin's chest and stood petrified with astonishment as if they were seeing a miracle. It was incredible. When the clouds retreated for a short while, a thin mist spread from that part of the shirt and would leave a dry patch on his chest, with uncertain borders.

Finally, the governor, who consulted the palace's chief teacher, judges, astrologers, and court clerks, decided to untie Muhyettin's neck from the rope before the third day. The square was evacuated with much difficulty. The four guards under the supervision of the Head Jailor brought him down with great fear and took him to the observatory building at the far end of the square. Not a single servant of Allah touched the corpse that was stretched on the stone floor with its completely soaked shirt on it, except for the part that came right on top of the chest. Until the governor came and ordered the Head Jailor, the secret of Muhyettin remained with him, lying on the ground. When the Head Jailor lowered the shirt to the waist at the order of the governor, those who were there snapped to attention on the left chest with great curiosity. They looked closely, but they could not see a single mark, stain, or any other sign. It was just like any human body that lay before them, with a pale skin that had not seen the sun in a while.

The distinguished minds of the state waited hopelessly in front of the dead body. The rain outside poured heavily again. They became a little encouraged with the sound of the rain behind them and with that courage they initiated a discussion among themselves. They then decided that the surgeon should cut open Muhyettin's chest and examine it. Right at that moment, the madman came inside unnoticed and curled up in a corner. Then getting up from his place the madman began to writhe and convulse as if he had jumped into a fire. They could understand only one of his jumbled sentences with clarity:

'Do not harass the chest of the innocent anymore.'

13

THE PALMS OF MAJNUN NURETTIN

In the beginning, no one called him by the name 'majnun'. Nurettin Farisi was his name – the sole heir of a well-to-do family, the indulgent husband inclined to his wife's comfort, the sweet-natured father of his children, and the master of his household, Nurettin. In the summer months that left everyone drenched in perspiration, carefree Nurettin dozed off next to the fountain in the garden of his mansion, located to the west of the city of Kazvin. In the winter months, he got lost in himself while smelling fragrant frankincense near the brazier in the huge gallery. The world was so distant to Nurettin that even the gathered dirt in human hair would not come near him. Of course, no one could imagine that one fine day Nurettin would transform into a big ball of fire from inside.

This change did not happen suddenly, as others who saw from outside would perceive. It took months for this simple question, which tripped his thoughts and wandered around the bends of his mind for a long time, to take the shape of a large, crooked hook. Nurettin's wife did not make a fuss over her husband's gradual deteriorating peace of mind, thinking that this was one of those situations a man got into once in a while. His friends thought he went into a reverie during their conversations as a result of some kind of a quarrel between him and his wife. His children thought this to be an unresolved issue between their father and his friends.

All this time, the distance between Nurettin and his life was getting wider steadily. While reflecting, 'Let me just find the

59

answer to the question I am pursuing,' he did not even realize that he had started to tear the veil that protected a man from inquests. The question that meddled with Nurettin's mind came to him one afternoon.

That afternoon, when he had opened his palms while praying on the prayer rug, which had been weaved painstakingly with fine embroidery and its threads dyed with Turkey red, he saw suddenly that his palms were completely empty. For a little while he watched his hands, which he opened towards the sky five times a day, as if they belonged to a stranger. He watched them and was stunned. Which prayer had seen his palms worthy of it until now? Even after giving it much thought, he could not find a single prayer of his that had risen up to the skies intensely. The indistinctiveness of his prayers, the lifelessness of his passions, and the banality of his expectations bothered him. 'What is it, I wonder?' he asked himself.'What is it actually in the palms of so many people who get lost in themselves while praying with their hands open?'

Maybe this was just one of the countless questions that got caught up in the minds of a good number of people. If he wanted to, he could have let himself fall into the well of forgetfulness at that moment and return to his own world, to his garden, and to his mattress under the shadow. But he did not do that. He asked himself a question and took the answer to this question very seriously. Nurettin set out into the life of another Nurettin, whom he never knew. Leaving his sweet wife, whom his mother chose for him with great efforts, his three children, who were born one after another, his rich inheritance with which he could get by until death without ever having to do anything, the conversations full of his friends' jokes, and the soft mattress on which he sat with pleasure. When Nurettin took the road from Kazvin, the Walled City was still very far off from the Majnun, who would become an essential part of its square.

Nurettin, who went out of the big door of his mansion towards life, along with his question, passed through the bazaars that were crowded by people with their bodies, breaths, and gaze. He passed through the open secrets of the middle-class neighbourhoods, smoky and dingy places that would make someone faint, where people hardly knew their way through the lamps of learned men and the wits of disciples that would disdain books. He passed through the heat of a new corpse and the chill of the cemeteries. He passed through all the ages of human beings, all the completely different-from-each-other demeanours of every age, workings of every day, ennui and expectations. He visited secluded mosques and sometimes he became a guest in the dervish lodges built on the mountain edges. He did not get tired of going back-and-forth between two distant cities, while travelling with camel caravans. As his path lengthened, so did the path of the question in his mind. He exposed the fear that one got from the inside of his palms with the courage of another. He brought anticipation side by side with gratitude and compared desire with austerity. The more he paid attention, the more the palms increased in number and the people hiding behind their palms were countless.

What he learnt from the palms of those who prayed in whispers opened the doors of those who prayed in silence. After a while, he could understand the colour of the wishes by looking at how the people opened their palms. He was able to decipher what people begged for by the way they sat, the way they extended their arms, the way their waists bent, and the way their fingers were entwined into each other. He became an expert in distinguishing the secrets of people by looking at their postures when they left their houses. What not did they hide in their palms – the servants, who constantly praised their masters, were actually hiding their hatred for them. The honest were hiding their betrayals that no one knew; the reliable people, their countless lies that they told. The people whom everyone loved very much were hiding their lovelessness towards them; friends, their betrayals to each other. The murderers were hiding the blood in their hands; sinners, an innocent garden. The heroes were hiding their cowardice; the wise ones, the height of an easy obstacle. Poor people full of pride were hiding a cruel affluence; dwarfs were hiding height; ugly were hiding beauty, and the old were hiding the art of living. Nurettin saw many palms, opened to the sky and countless prayers hiding in them.

He walked from palm to palm, just like a cloud of dust, as he could not take his mind off the question that had entered his psyche. And with the secret of every palm that he solved, he saw that the distance between the people and their conscience kept on increasing. He saw that there was a thick lining present under the apparent lives of men, which no one could catch sight of. People were using their clay-bodies just like armour. They were using this armour and filled everything they hid from others, inside it. When that armour became full to the brim, they then needed some expansion and mostly at this moment, they opened their hands to the sky. Because everyone carried another world, another desire, a different individual inside them, life turned into a shrewd game with its real face hidden meticulously.

What he saw shook Nurettin's confidence in his outlook towards the world. The nickname 'majnun' got attached to him after he started speaking publicly about the things people hid inside their clay. It was as if he was a mirror now, and whatever stumbled upon him, gave itself away.

14

THE FOOT IN THE STIRRUP

Believing that he could make his own horseshoe, shoe an animal without hurting it, and perform many other skilful acts of horseshoeing, his master decided that it was time for Fettan to become a master like him. He would announce this at the 'girding of the loincloth' (to finish one's apprenticeship, become a master workman) ceremony held on the third Friday of June. This ceremony had been held without interruption since the times of His Holiness Abdulkasim, the patron saint of horseshoers. In the horse square, the ironsmiths, tinsmiths, coppersmiths, horseshoers, and other professionals gathered and cauldrons were put on stoves. Food was cooked, tables were set up, wrestling matches were held, and later in the afternoon, the ceremony of girding of the loincloth, which the apprentices looked forward to with excitement, was held.

When that day came, Fettan's master, like all other masters, stood up with pride and said, 'My apprentice has become a master now.' Like all apprentices, Fettan, blushing with embarrassment, kissed the hand of his master, who girded the loincloth on him. With great care, he shoed his first horse and proved his mastery to the attentive crowd. He was appreciated for his skills and made his master proud. He felt a sense of superiority in himself as he left the square.

Everyone feels this superiority inside once they become a master. But if Fettan felt that grandness, his mother almost felt like putting on wings and flying high in the sky. I will not say anything – you decide for yourself whether this was just the joy of a mother, arising from the knowledge of her son becoming a master or something else.

If you want, you can raise your eyes and take a look at the festive square that is about to disperse. Do you see a larger body than Fettan's among the ironsmiths, coppersmiths, groomers, herders, saddle-makers, women, and children? Of course, you don't. Also, look at the smiling woman sitting next to him, about whom it is difficult to decide whether she is his mother or his child. Look, mother and son are sitting side-by-side. Look at Fettan, no, wait, Master Fettan now, who is big enough to scare those who do not know him but his demeanour near his mother is that he would get frightened if someone yelled at him. This is so because the soul of this giant of a human, of this man who has the most sculpted body in the city, did not grow with his ever-growing physique. Fettan became a man, but his soul remained a child. As he got older, there grew an emptiness inside him that produced hollow sounds upon being touched.

Soon the new master and his tiny mother will arrive home, a dinner table will be set up, and the most delicious dishes will be put in front of him. Fettan will be so happy that he will barely fit in the door of the room where his bed is laid. The bed would have been prepared by his mother with much care and who knows, with how many sheep's wool rugs. He will stretch across his soft bed and close his eyes. As soon as he closes his eyes, the grandness he felt inside him and this long day will both be asleep along with him. And, when he wakes up in the morning, he will get up as Master Fettan for the first time, go out of the house as Master Fettan, and will go to his Master Fettan horseshoe shop, which he opened with his master's help and was adjacent to his master's shop.

But today, as soon as Fettan closed his eyes, someone knocked the door of his dreams. When he looked up and saw the guest, he started perspiring. He was at his wit's end. He could not find his hands and join them in front, could not think properly as to how he should show his respect. Fortunately, the patron saint of horseshoers, His Holiness Abdulkasim, was a man of experience. The master of masters was watching the great Fettan, who had now entered the crowning circle of his profession, with a smile on his face.

'Don't worry,' he said. Fettan stopped worrying.

'Relax,' he said. Fettan became relaxed.

'Sit down in front of me,' he said and Fettan followed.

The patron saint of horseshoeing, His Holiness Abdulkasim, of course, had come to see his horseshoe shop that would be opened in the morning and pray for him before anyone else. Master Fettan was delighted. He was very delighted. He came to his senses quickly. But the nails and the horseshoes that he fixed started to fall on the ground. Still the patron saint did not say, 'This is not the way a master works, Fettan.' He let it go and smiled. Then he looked around. He looked at the horseshoes and pegs. He took the hoof-cutting blade, scraper, and the pincers one by one in his hand and examined them. He changed the places of the stapler and the nail file. He took the anvil and put it next to the hammer. The young master was ecstatic as he watched Master Abdulkasim giving life to all his belongings by touching them. But suddenly something happened. Master Abdulkasim frowned and looked sharply at Master Fettan. He asked, 'What is this woman stirrup doing here?' Let alone answering, Fettan began to melt with fear in front of the master and found his way out by waking up. When he woke up, under the influence of this unexpected great visit, he imagined the quilt he slept under to be his shop that had collapsed upon him. He searched for its door for some time. Finally, when he managed to stand up, he took a deep breath. A deep breath and an anxiety that ruins one's morning.

Fettan, who was woken by his mother every morning, left the house before his mother could wake up. The haste in his walk worried even Majnun Nurettin, who held the watch of the square at night. At a time when the night's black thread and its white thread start separating themselves, he went inside the shop which was to be inaugurated. Until the sun came up, he tried to find the stirrup that had made Master Abdulkasim angry. He searched for it all over and then searched again – it was not there anywhere.

The masters who gathered to open his shop with good prayers found him drenched in sweat. They looked into his eyes with curiosity and thinking it to be the excitement of being a new master, they did not ask him anything. They found it appropriate to act as if everything was normal. Finally, they did the inauguration of the horseshoe shop and Fettan shoed his first horse at his own shop that morning. He hit the nail with some restlessness in him. He hit the nail, trying not to show the trembling hands to his master.

This restlessness continued for three months. After three months the traces of his dream were erased by time. Horses went, horses came. The seasons bid farewell to other seasons. Fettan's horseshoe shop got established. This happened thanks to that great force he seemed to possess. The horses he grabbed from the hoof not only stopped moving, but went down on their knees and remained on the ground. All the excitable horses of the city were referred to him. People were amazed by the strength of his wrists, his skill in shoeing horses, and in his posture, which was like a big nursing home, when he did his job.

Fettan's peace of mind was spoiled late in the morning in the seventh year of horseshoeing. He was sitting in front of the door and shaving the horseshoes that he had bought and then got cut from Ironsmith Rifat. Suddenly, a horse came and stood in front of him. He looked at the horse which was standing still. He saw a rather small stirrup that dangled from the horse's flank. He saw a shoe made of gazelle skin and decorated with floral designs, which was even smaller than the tiny stirrup. He saw a foot inside the shoe that was even tinier than both the stirrup and the shoe. When he saw the tiny foot he felt a different kind of beating in his heart that he had never felt before.

Later, after a long time, he raised his eyes and planted them on the owner of the foot who was sitting on the horse. 'I am coming from Karabudunlar,' she said, in a voice that made the morning crack with envy. 'How good would it be if you shoe this horse before Sunday, Master Fettan,' she said. 'You don't know, everything is on my back,' she said and talked sweetly about her troubles. She spoke about the plains she was coming from. On her way back, she did not forget to say, 'There is no comfort for Aygül in this world.' After Aygül was gone, the fate that builds a third house out of two different houses kept swinging with a stirrup for days in the yard until Master Fettan opened his door.

On the first night of their marriage, Fettan searched for someone in the void inside him because that tiny foot had become a huge woman and sat in front of him. He just stood in front of the new bride on the edge of the bed and watched her like a stranger, just watched her. He looked at Aygül as an extension of the pretty foot he saw in the stirrup. Aygül too looked at him. She eyed her husband from head to toe with the grief of coming down from the slopes of the hills. In the body of this big man, who was curled up in the corner, just looking at her feet, was another man sitting, who did not disturb his peace, never lost the rhythm of his breath, and was unaware of the roads and the journeys he would take. Aygül understood this from the very first day. She spent the first week pitying Fettan, the second week as his sibling, the third week pouring out their grief to each other, and the fourth week saying good-bye to each other. At the end of the fourth week, Master Fettan had already started to sleep peacefully on the floor bed that his mother spread for him.

That night the patron saint of horseshoeing Master Abdulkasim came to visit Master Fettan once again. Once again Fettan was at his wit's end but did not do most of the clumsy things of his first dream. Nor was the patron saint of horseshoeing there for long. In a few sentences, he expressed his gladness for removing the woman stirrup that he had put in his shop. Just before leaving, he said that Konos Agha was waiting for him and gave the gift of smile to the master. Fettan got up from his bed with the fever of the order he received, and rushed to the derelict house of Konos, the Bandit, who did not open his door for anyone. After he entered inside, he found Konos lying near the burning brazier. He was dead. Horseshoer Fettan's job as the caretaker of the tomb began that day – for life.

15

THE BIRDCAGE OF
IRONSMITH RIFAT

Whenever Ironsmith Rifat passed through the neighbouroods, there would be eyes of countless women watching him from behind the old garden walls through the cracks where weeds began to grow. They thought of two things when they saw him – beauty resided in them and manhood in Rifat. Rifat passed through the deep sensual voices of desire, droopy glances, dusty passions, slender waists, and crystalline wrists. He passed them and went into his shop that was among the shops of other ironmiths. His was a totally different kind of lordship that succeeded to affix that unseen crowd hiding behind the windows, leaves, or walls, to himself just by walking down the road. He was married. But no one took notice that he was married. He was not young. But no one even thought about his age. He was tough. But everyone wanted his toughness to be directed to them. All of the five doors, which according to women could not be found in a single man, opened in Ironsmith Rifat – a calm face, a glance full of desire, a body that could provide shelter, a dominating intensity, and a femininity to have a heart-to-heart talk. It was as if his core was also processed with the iron that he processed. He had become an inscrutable man who processed the ore into iron, shaped that iron, and gilded it even some more. It was as if what the many years withheld from countless men, handed them over to Rifat.

The Rifat of the women and the Master Rifat of the men resembled two different persons passing through two separate paths and crossing the roads only once in a while. In the eyes of the men, Rifat was an unmatched man for three reasons – no one looked as good as him in what he did, no one was as good as him in what he did, and no one's fame spread out of the city as much as his. For example, Master Rifat's apprentices used to look at him as if he was the king of metals who could speak with the core of iron. He used his bellows, pincers, anvil, and his hammer in such harmony that it made people think of all these tools as parts of his body. This black, hard object called iron would move between different states of being and eventually take on a living form capable of speaking with men. Swords coming out of Rifat's hands, daggers pounded upon in Rifat's anvil, copper buckets carrying the echo of Rifat's hammer inside them, spread a proud glow around. Rifat knew not only the art of casting iron, but also its history. He had three great masters – Prophet David, an anonymous ironsmith who managed to melt the iron of a mountain to save his ancestors when they were trapped, and Kaveh the blacksmith who dethroned the cruel Zahak. In Rifat's eyes, iron was the womb of the earth and the mother of all metals. It was the life inside of life that took shape between the anvil and the hammer. Already in *Cevahirname*, which describes the precious stones, it was written that iron was feminine in nature. That is why Rifat used to touch iron as if it was a woman. That is why the iron he touched was sold in the bazaars of distant cities, stored in the kitchens of distant houses, and was carried on the waists of soldiers of distant lands.

Women dreamt of having all the five doors present in Rifat open towards them. The men coveted the three doors of his mastery. But the forty-two-year-old Rifat had one strange rule that nobody could get to its core – he would not make a birdcage. He would not even blow once into a fire in which iron for a birdcage was to be melted. Even for once his anvil would not lay the red hot metal for it. He would not tire the back of his hammer for this job and he would not pour water on the iron for this work. People sometimes thought that there was a secret gateway between that indescribable charm of his and his insistence on not making cages for birds. In this respect, women found a breezy look in him that would challenge the heaviness they felt in their chests. Men believed this rule to be the code that was the result of his knowledge of substances.

No matter who commented what on this matter, Rifat's insistence on not making a birdcage was a fertile question mark that increased the curiosity of the people every day. The more they became curious, the bigger became the question mark; the more it was unanswerable, the larger it grew. The more Rifat remained silent, the more colossal it became. After a while, this question mark started to make anxious those who had pet birds. Weird suspicions began to develop in those who wanted to make cages for their pet birds. They tried to find a clue by putting many stories about the birds in the cages, into the birdcages that Ironsmith Rifat did not make, but to no avail. They tried to find the answer in Fariduddin Attar's book *Mantiq-ut-Tayr*, but to no avail. They could not open the secret of Rifat by opening the cage where he had kept the secret.

One day they came across an answer they never expected. The answer they came across suddenly tripled the number of secrets.

Rifat's fate changed when he was forty-two years old. When the Ironsmith reached that age, a crack that had not been seen by anyone occurred in his torso, which looked like a rich mineral deposit. A goldfinch entered through that crack and asked to make a house for her from the cage that he withheld from everyone. Neither his wife nor his apprentices nor those who had tried to reach the ninth door, which is full of secrets, by opening the first eight of Rifat's doors, realized that eight of Rifat's doors were opened by someone among them and someone among them stood at the threshold of the ninth door. However, Rifat, who passed through the sounds of grief in the neighbourhoods, was not the same Rifat for a long time now. Rifat, who was greeted sincerely upon reaching the square, was also not the same Rifat! Even though no one noticed, a hidden miniature painting was added to the hilt of the swords he made, he started to hear the echo of his insides in the copper buckets he made. The fire he had bellowed and the iron he had set on fire was now himself.

For Rifat, the journey of loving a woman did not take too long. Gülzade, who managed to extend the tongs to his heart, wanted to see for sure whether the melting thing was the essence of his own iron in the furnace of Rifat, whom countless eyes had marked and who had a wife at his home. She wanted that there should not remain any doubt that the Rifat who flared the fire with the bellows was the Rifat who glowed together with her. Master Rifat was quick to understand which door this capricious goldfinch wanted to open. He quickly understood two more things. A clear boundary line appeared in Gülzade's eyes that wanted to distinguish herself from other women and she was willing to look into the well of death that proved her uniqueness rather than remain in the garden of ambivalence. Rifat understood that the only way to save the bird named Gülzade from the cage she had fallen into was to make a cage for this bird.

Finally, Master Rifat started making a cage one evening. He started to make it after sending away all his apprentices. He started to make the bars of the cage by putting life into the fire with the bellows and with the fire, into iron, then resting all of them with water. The darkness of the night stretched between Rifat and the birdcage he had started to make.

When his apprentices came in the morning and opened the door, they were baffled by what they saw. Countless birds fled through the door, many of whom they could not even recognize. When the apprentices entered the forge from where the birds had come, they found a birdcage in the middle and, near the birdcage, they found the corpse of their master who had been pecked to death by the birds.

16

THE HERBALIST WHO DIED BETWEEN LAUGHS

Herbalist Yusuf, who saved lives using bitter herbs, was the most loved among the three perfumers of the city. Discomforts, diseases, and pains used to open his door the most. There were three reasons for his popularity – his father, his discretion in keeping a secret, and Charming Makbule.

His father, who wanted his son to continue with his profession, had him removed from his friends and games at a young age and tied him to this house of pains. In the beginning, Yusuf insisted on not entering the shop, where countless scents made the atmosphere heavy. He whined and even kept on crying. But adroitly, his father succeeded in incorporating him among the colourful spices, bitter roots, and dried leaves.

For the next fifty-two years, Herbalist Yusuf entertained grievances from all kinds of persons. He learned about the pains from the people and about the remedies from his father. He experienced the incapability of finding a cure for expiration from this world among his scents, and then he completely took over the counter of the shop. Time brought new diseases to him and taught him to find new remedies. Just like his father, he welcomed all his customers as gently as possible and sent them off the same way. He never forgot that people were looking for solace even in a glance from him.

The Herbalist did not forget one thing – keeping the secret of the suffering. He never carried grievance into grievance, awkwardness into awkwardness, and shame into shame. It was as if under his soft skin there was a thick armour that kept the secret of many people. The intimate aspects of many of the people walking around the streets of the Walled City, in the neighbourhoods, and inside the houses were recorded in his tender gaze. Sometimes he played a game with himself, wearing the secrets left to him, watching the city with those eyes. For example, he made the street-sweeper Müştak, who used to boast about his masculinity, change places with the depressed Müştak, who was looking for remedies for his impotence. He constantly made the herdsman Kadri, about whom everyone was curious about what he talked when talking to himself all the time, chat with the three female djinns who imposed themselves on him for years now. Freckled Rasime, who made hearts stop with his physique, was afflicted with such a hairy body that even the epilating wax could not do any good to him. He did not leave a single spot in his skin to be peeled off to get rid of those hairs. The pretty wife of the first clerk of the governor managed to bury two of her foetuses without his knowledge. Despite Yusuf's response 'It is a sin' to all her suggestions, she persisted in procuring the medicine for dropping the next foetus. When Herbalist Yusuf looked at the Walled City with its secrets, he saw a completely different population who polished their pearls, whose baldness overflowed its turban, who had clogged stones in its urinary tract, whose breasts did not produce milk, who fell in love with the wives of others, who suffered from tuberculosis, or who lost their minds at full moon. At the end, he would be grateful for the good and healthy ones being more in number, close the window of secrets, and feel relieved.

It was not her charm that attracted Charming Makbule to Herbalist Yusuf, but her femininity. One afternoon, when she entered with her familiar laughter and assuredness of middle-age, the Herbalist was preparing medicine from absinth for Bahtiyar, who could no longer put a bridle on his lust. Makbule looked at the Herbalist, with a radiant gleam in her eyes. With some urgency, she inquired about his health and family first. After eyeing the lecherous Bahtiyar, who was standing in a corner, from head to toe, she pretended that she had not seen him at all and started looking at the herbs in the shop like horsetail, milfoil, fennels, and jujube. Herbalist Yusuf quickly understood that Makbule was waiting for Bahtiyar, who had harassed his wife with his lust, to leave.

Finally Bahtiyar was gone and Makbule started talking. She was getting old! Unlike the people's legends about her beauty, the years had already started to diminish some things in Makbule. Her skin had dried up. She was not able to hide the dark circles under her eyes. She could not maintain the softness in her hands anymore. While she was mentioning all this, she remembered to ask Yusuf, whose wife died four years ago, whether loneliness was difficult. That day, the Herbalist prepared a skin cleanser from rosewater for her. He also gave her jasmine oil for her shrivelled skin and coriander oil for the dark circles under her eyes. Loneliness and beauty were together now. Makbule kept talking about the youth-giving oils of Herbalist Yusuf to the countless women who came to her house. And, on every visit, the Herbalist told her about the mixtures he prepared only for her.

When time moved loneliness and beauty from just being profitable partners and made them each other's confidant, it was time for the Herbalist to make a wish – the Herbalist wanted to fill the vacant place of his deceased wife. Half of his bed of habits had been empty for four years but the Herbalist had not lost his power, as it seemed. Charming Makbule, the only living fountain in that lifeless city, could well have one of the women, who came to her with their bowls to fill them with joy, married off to him. Undoubtedly, it was unimaginable that the woman he wanted could be as beautiful as Makbule. What the Herbalist wanted from Charming Makbule, a woman worthy of palaces, was to recommend a woman who would be worthy enough to sit beside Charming Makbule. Charming Makbule realized instantly that this desire of marriage, while brushing her aside with praises, was based on the future of her beauty. Without revealing the chill inside, she broke into one of her familiar laughter and asked, 'Is there any dearth of women for the Herbalist?' Then she went away from the shop and the marketplace immediately. For Charming Makbule, this was as easy as peeling two garlic cloves and bringing them together. And she would do that. Her heartache was that she was only the Charming Woman (Dilber) of everyone's desire, but not accepted (Makbule) to anyone's love.

Despite all his understanding, the Herbalist could not become aware of the hurt in Makbule's voice and the pain in her smile, and not even her hurried departure.

It was the beginning of summer when Herbalist Yusuf was married off by Makbule, who tried so hard to protect her beauty. Dürdane, who would fill the empty space of his first wife, entered the house with lime fragrances. And from the very first day she started to pull the days of death of Herbalist Yusuf towards herself. The old Herbalist became more and more distracted and a little more irritated with every passing day after that night. Only Makbule knew what went inside the house that night. Some tied it to be the deadness of the city that made everyone go out of their wits, some to the moodiness of his new wife. And others said that it was because the soul of his ex-wife, who was of a very affectionate character, had not left his house yet. In the days when rumours permeated to all the herbs in every part of his shop, the Herbalist did not busy himself with gossip, but in doing two important things. First was to prepare the beauty oils for Makbule for keeping his secret and the second was the elixir of youth to repair his old age. By obtaining unseen mixtures from unusual herbs, he tried his best to delay the first as much as possible and revive the second as soon as possible. In the third month of his new marriage, he poured the last syrup made by trial-and-error method on his head, felt the buzzing of his blazing blood, and quickly set out for home.

That night, the essence of the countless herbs that he tried on his body for three months, leaked out of his mouth and nose like soup. Dürdane laughed out aloud at the bedside of the man who had summoned his youth.

17

CHARMING MAKBULE

Do not think that Charming Makbule is someone who likes to gossip. Although the name of every street in this city is remembered by my name, nobody knows that I keep silent about much more than I talk about. If I have intervened and taken the mike from the author, there are many reasons and I think you too will approve of them. Do you think I don't know what's on your mind because of the lightness in my name?

Had I not been compelled to, of course, I would not have allowed my name to be the common name to represent all the women each of you dreams about in different ways. I do not know but maybe to entrap Charming Makbule, who was sitting in her place in a decent manner, this writer used my name in some parts of his stories, with stains on it. He doesn't look like an innocent person at all. Either he is provoking me to tell him the secrets of the Walled City he couldn't learn about, or he is trying to make space for telling about my end in the same merciless way he told about the end of these innocent acquaintances of mine.

Has anyone succeeded in deceiving Charming Makbule ever? Then how can she be deceived now? This writer and I have already made a deal between us – I will give him a few hints about his protagonists when he starts to get lost among their mysterious destinies. He, in turn, will not keep the secret of my end from you but will not reveal the identity of my lover, about whom I'll give you some hints soon. I think this is a good deal for both of us. Thanks to this agreement, your writer, who was desperate to finish his stories, will finally survive the Walled City. As for me, I will be able to keep the same beautiful Charming Makbule in your imagination by hiding my end from you. Because with an undisclosed love, nobody can kill a beauty whose end is unclear.

And since he swore not to interfere with what I have to say, I want to say a few things about what I think about this author. I'm sure that if anyone among you knows him, you must think that he is a shy man who minds his own business. I wish that was true. At the very first meeting, I immediately saw that rakish gleam that scattered from his gaze. While sitting and talking beautifully about the Walled City, he sometimes spoke so sweetly that I had difficulty in keeping my mind from getting distracted. I have seen many people like this and dealt with them easily. What does this man think he is? Does he think that he will enter in my good books by putting two words together? If my heart opened just by someone putting a few words together beautifully, I would have become the servant of so many by now. Even two of the five gates of Ironsmith Rifat are hard to find in him. I have been a guest at his home thrice, and each of the three times a dishevelled man greeted me, who did not know what he was doing. His whole existence would not be worth more than the collet of Charming Makbule's ring.

Nevertheless, it's not that I did not like some of his traits. Either Allah knows or I, about how much effort he has put in trying to find and reveal the coquettish Walled City, which is gone forever and even a single debris of its ruins is not left. Okay, he doesn't have the handsomeness of Master Rifat, who is desired by so many women, but I will not hide a quality that I have seen in this writer, similar to what men found in Rifat. When he writes, he gets lost in himself as if he is in love. Many of you would not know, but I have observed him to be a very patient man. There may be a secret in him, just like Rifat had one. I'm afraid that his end might be similar to Rifat's. Anyway. Before this Tahir, may his tongue get cut off, says something about me to make people think unnecessary things about me and before you too ask, 'Well, who are you, Charming Makbule?' let me start with my own story.

Look, even I said Charming Makbule so many times while talking about myself. But this is not my real name. There were three people in the world who knew my real name; all three have migrated from this world. My parents died later, his death

77

happened very early. You will find neither my mother's nor my father's story in what you read, as this writer is only curious about those with bad ends. But my friend is here, among the pages of this book, along with me. I told you that I would give you a hint about him, but I am not sure yet. When he died, he suffered so much that I forgot the days he loved me and kept the vigil of his pain. You will never hear his name from me. Do not think that I am doing this to make you wonder. If you saw a single point of the place he was holding in my heart, you would understand what I mean.

Still, people are related to other people's suffering. Not by reading the story of Charming Makbule, but by listening to the simple story of her murdered lover, I know that you will understand who he was. I have only one request from you – keep it a secret. Keep it a secret so that those countless people, who are far from the manners of how to talk about two lovers and their love, should not learn about this. When the silk of the gentlemen falls into the market, it only gets hurt. Know this and it should be enough that under the tongue of Charming Makbule, whose beauty is legendary, remained hidden the name of such a brave man that neither moneylenders, nor merchants, nor the sons of the governor could touch it even slightly.

As I said, Dilber Makbule was my refuge, not my name. So that they are not offended, let me start with my parents first. I grew up in a wooden mansion in Isfahan. My father, who was a carpet merchant, and my mother, whose eyes sparkled when she waited for him every evening, raised me like a gift they presented to each other. I vividly remember many evenings my father reciting couplets from *Saadi Shirazi* and my mother lying down leisurely and with joy listening to his beautiful voice. They would start playing with me as soon as I woke up in the morning, taking me between them. They would flirt with each other while playing with me.

They never lost the enthusiasm on their faces for each other. As I grew up, they seemed to become childish. Being grown up is a feeling that you don't feel yourself as much as you are made to feel by others, and others determine your fate rather than you yourself. Others told me about the transition from a girl child to a young woman. When others said to my mother, 'What a beautiful girl she is,' I went up to the mirror and looked for my beauty. When they said, 'How much she has grown,' I closed the door of my room and admired my height, fineness of my waist, and my figure. Perhaps the secret of becoming a young woman is this – to cease to be the child of your parents and become the favourite of others.

My body did not let all these praises down. My beauty became more and more apparent as it was praised. When we went to the bazaars, when women praised me and men looked at me with desire in their eyes, it would not be a lie if I say that a heat that I cannot describe spread over me. But this was not because men looked at me; it was because men looked at me, and not at other women. This was one of my strongest knowledge that would make me 'Charming Makbule' in the future. We love a man more so that other women become jealous of us. So many suitors started to appear for me that I could no longer sit among the girls.

It seems as if a black curtain hangs in the luck-house of beauty. Whatever you do, it suddenly appears before your eyes at the mouth of your destiny, and you are not able to see what is in front of you. While I was wandering from tongue to tongue, wearing headdresses, silver tops, and swaddled apparel, important people from the Walled City came to our doorstep. I understood from the happiness on my father's face and the excitement on my mother's that they would cage their beautiful bird together. I cannot tell you how I suffered from this grievous emotional blow. I watched with desperation whatever was happening in front of me. The threads of each star wrapped around my neck at night. My girlhood and my beauty, both turned into ruins where I was a captive. I was betrothed, and I lost my thirst and hunger. Gifts came and I watched those gifts as if they were the shroud of the Azrael. But do not think that I was suffering. My lover, whom I could see but not get together with, if we got together then I could not look at him, if I looked at him then I could not smell him. He would go into ruptures and kept wandering around our house. How helpless, how devastated he was.

Whatever happened, it happened three days before my wedding. As I had a premonition about it, I was not surprised at the news. My darling took the road of the Walled City three days before my wedding. He went in front of the governor saying that he had brought news from the bride's side and put that man of dark laws down with his sword. They made him suffer very much. I came to the Walled City not as a bride but as the guardian of the grave of the man I loved. I watched his bitter death everyday from under my veil. Whatever I had was there. I could not leave the murderer of my beloved nor the murdered.

I am not going to talk in detail about my first days in this city in which all the stones had been marked with the traces of disappearance, why I did not return to my parents, how my parents lived after I left, and how they died. In this city I acquired my new name 'Makbule', and the people here saw me worthy enough to put Charming before it. So I became 'Charming Makbule'. Once you get a name like charming, you are sentenced to live by being divided into countless faces and countless bodies in the eyes of others as men often do not look at the woman, but the image of that woman that they dress her with. As you can see, I heard about so many Charming Makbules that I was also surprised at most of them. Charming Makbule was described so much that even I could not recognize her anymore.

While I have a single mole on my neck, which no one had been fortunate enough to see, women talked about many moles on my neck. Even though I did not wear an anklet even once, they talked about how beautiful it looked on my ankle. They put Charming Makbule in the houses of people she had never known. They put her inside the doors that she never entered. All these stories made me happy instead of making me sad or angry. I took the Walled City inside my fist. If this city burned one Charming Makbule, I too burned this big city down. I made all the women my confidantes. There was no secret that did not reach me, and there was no curtain that did not open to me. I covered my pain with the lining of rumours surrounding me, secrets that no one could know, and strange stories.

No one noticed that I was walking with a dead person under my cover. But to tell you the truth, I got used to this city the way I had got used to my act of burying my darling into the ground. Still, the fineness of my waist disappeared in this city. This city gave me the wrinkles on my face. I silenced the howl that appeared in the emptiness of my chest with the hubbub of this city. Was

I getting old? Sometimes I started to envy Charming Makbule, whose stories travelled all around the city. If I could not compete with her in beauty, then that would be my end. Don't you dare say, 'You have suffered so much, Charming Makbule, what will you do with this beauty?' I kept all my memories closely wrapped in her fine muslin.

I implied this at the beginning of my talk also. It is not my habit to ask more than what I want to learn or say more than I want to. Best of all, let me fulfil the promise I made to this writer who listened to me with all his attention and then stepped aside. If he has a method and a style, Makbule also has a method and style, according to her. Those who read the stories told by the author will think that in this big Walled City, only people with bitter ends and runaways live. I and many other people were surprised and sad to see the ends of these people, whom I knew as good persons, who became the victims of their misfortunes.

But why only these people? For example, did Saddle-maker Ismail, who does not think of anything other than his job, who never even hurt an ant, have nothing worth mentioning in his life? Would it be bad if Zekiye, who eats five meals a day at home, sweats those five meals down her neck, but does not worry about the world, takes her place among these stories? At least, the author could have included Zakir, the muezzin with the beautiful voice, somewhere in these stories. Let me say that I do not think that it is right to choose only those things that make men suffer, from among the silent housewives living their own lives, tinsmiths, cloth makers, old men, saddle makers, children in sound sleep, and those who marry and set up their houses. I want you to know that Charming Makbule, doesn't matter whatever happened to her, would have liked you to know the stories of the pleasures of getting a new slipper, the sherbets drunk on the dinner table, and the little joys of the young girls with their fiancés on the edge of the gardens.

If it were up to me, I would not have put the story of that Bedouin Traveller at the beginning of the book. But this writer spoke about him more than anyone else and even made him one of the two pillars of this book, alongside me. You cannot imagine how much I hate him. He made Mahinur, the second most-beautiful woman of the Walled City after me, fall in love with him

81

and then he went away, leaving her with a child in her stomach. How many times I told my sweet Mahinur, begged and insisted even, that the smell of the road would not come off this man? How many times I said that those who come from far away go far away, but to no avail. I did not understand what she found in this swarthy and skinny man who had no adventure except to set up his tent, far and near.

This is how women are, you know. They believe their beloved is better than everyone else. They believe that they will be able to change everything. And then they are left with no one and nothing, just like my snow white Mahinur. If she hadn't heard the twitch of the child in her womb that day when she was abandoned, Mahinur would have descended into the well of death while looking at the naked mountain opposite their home. Fortunately, the Almighty took pity on her at the nick of the time. I heard that after going away from here, the Traveller wrote a long travel book describing the places he travelled. I wish he had not written it. He showed the Walled City as a dilapidated city somewhere on the other side of the world, so that no one knew what he had done to my beautiful Mahinur. One who doesn't know the value of a woman will never know the value of a city!

Do not remind me of that Magician Seyfettin. In both cities, his black magic tent appeared in front of my destiny. His end also resembled his tent eventually. How enthusiastically I went to watch his magic when I heard that his magic tent was set up in Isfahan. I still remember I was wearing an almond-green dress and a matching headdress on top of that. I had just turned sixteen. I came back under a spell from the place where I had gone to watch magic spells.

I came eye-to-eye with my darling in front of that tent. You know what happens when an eye finds itself in one eye, and now you have already learnt what happened to me. When the show came to the Walled City, I did not even visit its neighbourhood. I heard from the people who went to see the magic show of Seyfettin that it remained unfinished, and also that my name was mentioned to arouse people's desire to see the show. Of course, they did not know that I had gone to their tent in Isfahan. They, like everyone else, found it profitable to take advantage of Makbule's fame. But no one could understand why the money they paid was given

82

back and the tent was closed. What's not to be understood in this? Seyfettin, the cunning Seyfettin, who had the skill of reading the eyes of everyone in his tent, came eye-to-eye with those two eyes in such a manner that their gaze made the magician get into a tizzy. When he realized that he could not continue, he gathered everything and went away hurriedly. In fact, it would not be true to say that he got lost. He wandered around the Walled City until he set up his tent for the second time. Sometimes he even came inside the city. Of course, Innkeeper Numan knew when he came and in which room he stayed. What I know is that until his last magic of burning himself, he wandered around the circles of those two eyes. It was a very bad end. Despite the deep scar that the black tent left in my memories, I felt very sorry for Seyfettin when I heard about it.

When I settled in Sur City, Bilge Mansur had already left the city. I never knew him. Sometimes I ask myself, 'What good would come out of this city where a Charming Makbule fills the place emptied by the Wise Mansur, for God's sake?' and amuse myself. But women and sages are very similar. Both of them feel with their hearts and do not work without consulting their minds. They both quickly get affected by everything and can predict what will happen long in advance. If Wise Mansur had not migrated, the light of that retreat would have fallen on us only from afar. About his student, they say that on the day he sent his teacher off, he settled down in his own house, and never came out to the bazaars of the city again. When I heard him say good things about me, I thought that in this city there was at least one house of mercy for us. Just think about it, while everybody concerned themselves with the mole and the body of Charming Makbule, the worthy man ordered, 'Do not bother the woman, who knows what heartache she must have?' to those who visited him. But who listens to his order?

It seems life is like a race that goes on between the bodies of women and the words of sages. Whichever one gets ahead, the harmony of the bazaars is shaped accordingly. I always prayed for the long life of my master, whose face I had never seen, whenever I sat in that house of mercy. If he leaves us, nobody will be left to compensate for the emptiness that will arise in us. There is nothing incomprehensible about this. Some people take much more space than their presence. In this city, Makbule has no friend more valuable than Mansur's student.

Just as I came from Isfahan and became the most famous belle of this city, Nizamettin also came from Merv and became the most popular moneylender of this city. Makbule danced to her heart's content in the weddings of all his three daughters. All the three daughters married the men they chose for themselves. They embraced what they chose and they bore children of the ones they chose. I was not surprised that the Moneylender married his daughters off in a way that everyone found inconvenient. This was for the reason that he had been unhappy. He did not like his wife, who had been brought by his mother as 'wife' and placed beside him, even as a little girl. They slept and woke up for years in a double bed, yet treated each other as an affliction. The moments when they got close to each other the most were the moments when the Walled City faced disasters. At the time of disasters people cannot find a cure other than snuggling into each other's warmth. So, the three daughters were the gifts of three successive disasters. Do not conclude that the Moneylender's wife was a nagging, quarrelling woman from what I am saying. Theirs was a quarrel in silence. They gave the greatest pain they could give to each other, preferring to keep quiet when they needed to speak. No one heard either of them saying a bad word to the other. In the same room, like two necks hung on one string of fate, they quietly waited for the passing days to kill them. Of course, the slender neck migrated much earlier. When their mother died, Nizamettin's youngest daughter had just started to say the word 'mother'. The Moneylender has seen more seasons of the world not only than his wife but also his peers. But what good would it do if he sees the end of the world before seeing Charming Makbule even once? I'll tell you the truth, I like moneylenders!

As a child, I had heard this from that sweet, kind-hearted father of mine. The Chinese said, 'Every person has two suns; one inside and the other outside.' Whenever I see this Hüsrev, this saying always comes to my mind. He has been lying in the dens of vices for years, he has been a slave to marijuana for years, and he passed years not seen by anyone. He resembled one aspect of my darling. I like Hüsrev like my child. Do not look at the years he spent in the dark corners, or at his eyes deep like a well.

84

Anyone who looks a little bit carefully can see an innocent nature hidden in the face of this child, which no wrong can erase. But this was seen most by Charming Makbule, who has got a bad reputation for herself. I always felt sorry for him, always. From a distance, I asked about his well-being from others and tried to see to his needs according to my capacity. And if someone did something to him, it would be a knot that nobody knew about, wrapped around my neck. I did not think even once that the sun in Hüsrev, whom people considered a rogue, a devious idler, was extinguished. Some people suffer from a torment that no one can understand. They cannot close the chasm between themselves and the world. They flutter like a fish looking for water. Hüsrev's wife was the youngest daughter of Moneylender Nizamettin. I only mediated the dream he had seen, and I managed to place the owner of this strange spirit behind that veil. Who could ever survive Charming Makbule's plans, so how could Hüsrev? I felt the end of some people inside me at times. Moneylender's sweet daughter, who was blessed by the Almighty, could see in the suitors sitting behind the veil the possibility of going astray, if given a chance. Hüsrev had already gone astray. When the young daughter asked, 'What did you bring me?' there was nothing left with the man sitting opposite her to give, other than silence. The sun inside him shone as he remained silent. Who wouldn't close her eyes to that sun? He was like a newborn child. After their marriage, he said to his wife, 'When I sat across you, a light fell inside me.'

If my heart had not been tied to the stones of a grave until it died, if my first love had remained light enough to welcome a second lover, be sure that I would have been devoted to Stableman Behram. Now I can hear you say, 'Charming Makbule, how could you chose a horse tamer when so many chieftains, clerks, craftsmen, and aristocrats were available?' It is easy to say this for those who do not know Master Behram, the light of the steppes. Whenever I see Behram going or coming from somewhere, I become sad that the Creator did not create me as a man like him. Sometimes, I secretly want to be one of the foals that were tamed by him. Horses and women are so similar that one who knows how to treat a horse well would definitely know how to treat a woman. But you see, the fate of my Master Behram did not share his mastery with anyone except horses. When he couldn't be

85

together with Mahinur, whom he loved very much, he turned to the governor's farm. He devoted himself to the foals to be trained and to the apprentices who would train the foals. On the farm, for years, he looked at the foals that had been taken away from their herds. He observed their swing, fine ankles, and sturdy hooves. He would stand up suddenly and stroke the mane of the foals. As if I don't know – he saw a part of Mahinur in every foal, her swing, her defiance. By the time Mahinur heard that Behram loved her, the Traveller had been married to his bride, who was the second most-beautiful woman after Charming Makbule. See, that Bedouin once again came in front of me! I often looked at Mahinur and Behram with two blue-blood eyes, created for each other but not to be with each other. Sometimes angels who kindle beauty with beauty can be very preoccupied!

I would have liked very much that Miniaturist Burhanettin made a picture of me. Then I could have hung my beauty at my bedside, and would have learnt who Makbule is in the eyes of a man. I don't know how other miniaturists are elsewhere, but Burhanettin's face is like a dimly-lit hall with light filtering through its domes. Whenever I came across him, I thought his eyes got a little smaller. I say I 'thought' because my sweet Mahinur was abandoned, not once, but twice. First, the Bedouin Traveller, whose name I had to make an effort to remember, left her, and then her father also after him. Her father had been wandering around like a shadow for years; obviously his mind was stuck with something. According to Mahinur, three days before he disappeared in thin air, he had seen his Master from Merv but found it appropriate to paint a picture before he left. During those three days, her father never came home at night, but only twice during the day. She saw her father more restless than she had never seen him. She felt a doubt inside her. Burhanettin even came to say goodbye the day he left the city. He set out without saying for how many days he was going and when he would return. Nakkaş Burhanettin left behind the picture that he completed on the last night before his journey and Mahinur hid it from everyone. She thought that all the secret of her father's absence and not returning was hidden in this last picture. Even though I wanted it fervently, she did not show it to her older sister, Charming Makbule, even once. It's not that I was not worried about her losing her mind saying that she would unravel the secret hidden in the picture one day. When we last met, she said that when she looked at a point for a long time where the colours are all mixed up, a female body appeared.

You know, the light in Sakine's eyes was sacrificed on a coincidence. When I say Sakine, do not think that I'm talking about someone distant. In the absence of Numan, who left the house in the morning and did not return until midnight, we two women whose houses were not very far from each other, used to do embroidery on the cloth of darkness. Some nights we would take a tour of the city with our tongues. Some nights Makbule told her of the different kinds of men. Some nights we sought compassion from each other, like two patients suffering from cold. Some nights we travelled back to our girlhood days and sang folk songs. As the time for Numan to come in the middle of the night approached, Dilber Makbule would get up and return to the memory of the dead she had extended inside her. She also handed over Sakine to the indifference of her husband, who turned her home into an inn.

If you asked me, 'What kind of a woman was Sakine?' I'd say, 'Just look into her eyes once and that is enough.' It was as if her eyes were two glowing amber stones. It was as if the sun circled around them and her lashes protected them like an umbrella. If the eyes were sea, people would have landed on the shore of that sea, and the edges of Sakine's eyes would have turned into the place of the Day of Judgement. Pain visits people from the door they like the most. It came to visit Sakine through her eyes. If that blind Numan looked at the most beautiful eyes of his wife with desire even once, his wife would not have felt the need to get the approval of other eyes about the beauty of her eyes.

Even if nobody else knew, Sakine knew well that it was her eyes that spoiled the magic of the Magician Seyfettin. On the day when the tent was first set up, a curiosity had hit her in the fairground where she had reached by coincidence. Saying, 'What will be shown, I wonder?' she went inside. Like all magicians, Magician Seyfettin would look into the eyes of those who watched so that his tricks were not understood. Seyfettin, who came eye-to-eye with so many eyes and considered them just as a simple veil for his tricks, for the first time looked into a pair of eyes and could not come out of those eyes. As I was told, Sakine became very happy that the tent of the magician folded up. Now you must have understood why the Magician always wandered in the inns of the Walled City, and why he came to Numan's inn sometimes in disguise. Moreover, it was not for nothing that on each visit, he rented the room of the inn that overlooked the house adjacent to the inn. Do not think that Sakine cheated on her husband. The Magician was happy enough to see the power of those eyes, that's all.

Charming Makbule is witness that Seyfettin's eyes and Sakine's eyes did not see each other until the tent was set up for the second time. Then, Seyfettin's coarse apprentices started making a fuss about the second show, 'The magician will make the last big magic he left halfway through earlier.' This time Sakine was there, not by chance but by choice. Her intention was not at all to beguile Seyfettin. She just wanted to see if the magic of the first time would be repeated again. To understand this, you need to know that women get attached not to a man, but to those who are attached to their own beauty. But Sakine experienced the devotion to the beauty of her eyes with such great pain that she could no longer carry those two eyes under her lashes. Why would a woman want her husband to see them for the last time before she killed her most beautiful parts?

On the days Konos remained totally uncommunicative and did not come down to the city, my eyes looked at the mountains like everyone else. I heard a lot of women, who got bored in the middle of the day, say, 'Bandit Konos also did not come today after all.' Even if sometimes I got angry at him that the Bedouin Traveller's roads turned into my Mahinur's misfortune, my anger went away quickly. To tell you the truth, I saw him as the other wife of Hüsrev who went up the mountains. At the end, both of them drowned in the light. Now it would not be right to talk offensively about this blessed person, whose tomb's caretaker is the big and burly Fettan. Maybe we women understood him more than the men. Whenever he landed in the city, he reminded us that this city had a life. As I said, women could feel that Konos came down to the city for some other reason, not with the intention of stealing. It was as if a very naughty child was wasting himself for us in the mountains, in the cold, in the dungeons, so that the city did not forget to play, and the city did not explode from boredom. Sometimes when we didn't hear from him, some old woman would say, 'Where did my son Konos get stuck, I wonder?'

Of course, these words were not incorrect. He was actually like a naughty son. How do you think he returned to his mountains again and again, even though he was caught, captured, and thrown into the seven-door prison of the governor? Why did Charming Makbule write pages full of heart-piercing letters to the Head Jailor Alemdar, who broke the rusty iron of the prison, if not to save him after the fifth time he got captured? To tell you the truth, Konos, who is now our enlightened master, never had in him the possibility of becoming a real bandit or anything like it. Both the Walled City and Konos relieved each other's shrinking souls for many years, pretending that the city was afraid and he was frightening. But just as no one knows the place of Konos in me, you will not know either. The secret that connects me to my enlightened master Konos is a small point that lies behind all that I have told. It is as if the light that called him to the path of enlightenment and the death that connected me to a grave came out of the same door.

As I try to keep the secret from you, it sets traps for me to come out in front of you. And why did the writer bring the story of Majnun Nurettin, not in any other place but right after Konos, who was the joy of our life earlier and then became our enlightened master? But Charming Makbule learned to play the game inside a game much earlier than him – he has no idea! One day I came across a book in Sakine's house, which a guest who had come to his inn gifted to Numan. I was so bored that I took the book with me to read and enjoy for a few days. Do not start thinking, 'Makbule, do you know how to read and write?' So many girls saw me putting henna in the ink pot and they too wrote letters coming out their hearts in a similar fashion. The book I started reading from boredom also mentioned an Indian prince who left all his wealth in his palace and retreated to the forests. He exchanged his richness with poverty, pleasure with misery, butter and honey with herbs and roots. The more his enthusiasm for the world died, the more his inside came to life. When I read the story of this nobleman, do you know who came to my mind first? Majnun Nurettin. Okay, I can hear you scolding your mind and saying once in a while, 'We share a secret with Charming Makbule. But there is no charming girl inside this charm.' But what he said when he was not mad but madly in love, he said exactly in the middle of the book. In my opinion, Nurettin sees many things that we cannot see. His eyes are closed when we look at him but other eyes have opened in him that we cannot see. No matter who says what, I am afraid of such men. If a madman is outraged or frustrated, and starts to say words that cannot even be uttered, somebody is tearing the fabric of humanity somewhere. Since my house is close to the square, I hear Nurettin crying, shouting, and insulting someone or something some nights when there is no obvious reason. I wonder, 'Who is doing what, from where are the arrows coming and getting stuck in Majnun's conscience?' How his crying robs me of my sleep, you cannot even imagine.

Horseshoer Fettan seems like the human form of the Walled City. Both are too feminine to be men and too masculine to be women. Just like this city, which resembles a child inside a huge body, Fettan too is a child who took refuge in his big body. The Creator made his body big so that no one could harm his soul, which will always be of a child. What an innocent mother Fettan has; she believes in everything said to her. Despite all her age, every time she goes out, she sweats profusely with anxiety, as if the laughing fairies have kept this tiny woman's face as their home. The innocence of Fettan comes from his mother and his hugeness comes from his father. The strange boy shoed so many horseshoes that he could understand the animals that he shoed just from their pasterns. Those who pay attention must have seen it already. While Fettan grasped the pasterns of some horses with brutal force, he would touch those of some animals softly, as if he was touching the wings of a bird. He would not want to hurt some foals, and decided how to act as soon as he looked at their pasterns. Actually, this was the most solid knowledge about life that my child-horseshoer had. When it came to beauty he understood about it from a beautiful hoof and a beautiful pastern. When he saw the delicate foot of Aygül in the stirrup and the snow-white ankle left open by her trousers, it stirred some threads of his sleeping masculinity. I am saying 'stirred' because that is how he felt. The main secrets of a man appear after marriage. Aygül had spent her childhood and girlhood on the slopes of the hills, and with her firm body, she was ready to take on the huge body of Fettan. The poor unfortunate came and went quietly. She did not utter a single word about her husband who could not be a husband. In fact, had his mother not said, 'Come on, boy. Gather yourself and come,' she could have played his mother until death.

Now, Fettan is the caretaker of the tomb of my enlightened master Konos, the Bandit. He waits for a piece of Makbule's secrets there. There are so many doors in the world. One who cannot lie down with a woman, gets a place open for him next to a dead. Who else than this Makbule knows that Aygül, who got married to her cousin after getting separated from Fettan, goes to the tomb of Konos every week, hiding behind her veil and without showing herself to Fettan, leaves clean laundry and food for him? We went to the tomb together once. I cannot forget what she said on the way, 'Oh, how does it matter, whether he loved just a part of my foot or he loved the whole of me, Charming sister-in-law? I accepted that he loved me.' If anyone could understand how I got attached to the ground of a dead, it would be compassionate Aygül. Who knows, maybe she already has!

Oh, that Ironsmith Rifat! Oh, the Rifat, eight doors of whom opened for people and the ninth for death. Okay, Charming Makbule couldn't fit Stable Behram according to the place, but when it comes to Rifat, he is already dead and there was even a relapse in his chest. Who wouldn't want to be a sword or a dagger processed by him? Let me tell you, from the beginning itself I never liked Gülzade. Whenever we sat in the same assembly, the skirt of one of us would always take too much space the way it was spread. She oiled the beauty spot on her cheek so that she looked more beautiful, wore a corset so that her waist looked slimmer, and applied many perfumes she bought from the Herbalist Yusuf. And wherever we met, she would ask me loudly, 'How are you, elder sister Makbule?'

When I settled in the Walled City, Gülzade was still a small girl. People mistook her to be an elegant woman. What elegance? The best she could do was to become a waitress. Do you think that she did not know that it would be the end of Ironsmith Rifat when she asked him to build a birdcage? She sent her lover to death knowingly. I have no doubt about it. Gülzade, who put out his bellows, made such a request from Rifat and said, 'But I'll only believe you, if you die.' You all must be thinking that I am saying all this because I do not like that dried up cypress of a woman. If she had half the knowledge of Makbule, she would have known about the essence of iron. The ore of iron was lowered from the sky – only real ironsmiths know this. Rifat also knew. Does the sky ever imprison the sky? Would Rifat ever make a cage from the iron that came from sky to imprison a bird that flew to the sky? But he did. He did it for Gülzade. Who knows how much he must have looked in her eyes to convince her to give up her insistence? They say that the birds still hover around the grave of Ironsmith Rifat. On the day the women of the city heard that Ironsmith Rifat was dead, something went missing in them. You don't know, but looking at that something also gives hope. His passing through the street used to fan the wish of someone that he should never die. Do not say, 'What is this wish, Charming Makbule?' If you are a man, you will not understand and if you are a woman, you will not ask.

Why should I hide from you that I go to that fancy shop of Herbalist Yusuf? In fact, the first time I went, I did not know whether to laugh or go out of the shop. Why would that be? Because of Bahtiyar. When I entered, Yusuf was making a medicine to reduce his virility that he thought he hid from everyone. Would I go in if I knew he was there? Just think, Charming Makbule and Bahtiyar in the same string! As soon as I saw him, there was fire in my eyes. At the same time, I was sad. His wife remained like garbage from the noise of the blood of this crazy person. Whenever his name was mentioned all the women would chuckle and all the girls became curious. Thankfully, the Herbalist was an experienced man. He sent Bahtiyar off politely. After he went, Makbule's eyes released a sigh of relief. Please, you should not get deceived by this author. I did not go to the Herbalist's shop either for the wrinkles on my face or my dry skin. Like every woman, I was in search of a good perfume. And, while I was at it, I thought I also should benefit from this Herbalist's legendary pharmacy.

But who knew that I would be paying such a heavy price for it by being the talk of the town? Please know that I had nothing to do with the stated crime or complicity in Yusuf's taking Dürdane as his wife. Everyone goes shopping with their friend. Then how should I be held accountable that I went into the Herbalist's shop with Dürdane once or twice? Dürdane is a beautiful, statuesque, and assertive girl. Those who watch her walk think of a horse's amble coming from the meadow. I said so many things to the Herbalist like, 'You are old, this does not suit you,' but it is difficult to make a man, who has crossed forty and whose eyes are still caught in the gardens, listen. Actually, in the beginning, that owner of the house of pain and aches had thought of asking for my hand. When he did not see any response from me, his eyes shifted to my friend. I wish he hadn't done that. He asked for his humiliation himself. After getting married, he started looking for herbs that would bring strength to his knees and boiled the essence of unknown flowers. Now you tell me, how can the essence of flowers benefit someone whose essence has already dried up? Poor Dürdane. She didn't know what to do when the Herbalist was taking his last breaths. She came close to losing her mind then. She started laughing that night after not knowing what to do. This Walled City is like this. Loneliness gets so much into the deepest parts of people's souls that it is very difficult to say who would do something somewhere at some point of time.

This writer has made me tired. He made me tell in six hours what he wrote in six months. Actually it is good that it happened; thus the skill of the skilful came to light. After me, the story of this Tahir, whose tongue should be cut, and the story of the clerks of the good-hearted Governor Tuğluk, will be told. If you think that there is anything left to read after Dilber Makbule, then read! I have only one fear. The author has deliberately left Tahir behind me for him to tell the story of my pathetic end. Do not think that I trust him for giving me his word that he will not do so. Isn't the tongue of a man something that is prone to change easily? Charming Makbule, whose story has been told from the beginning till the end, has a small request from you – that you understand that the writer did not manage to tell all the stories properly. I came here just because the man I loved, who was killed mercilessly, was in this book. You too read his story, and you too were surprised at his death. Do not reveal the secret that Charming Makbule did not tell anyone. But you will surely find out the story of which he is the protagonist. If you cannot, you will not be able to see the colour of pain that consumed Makbule for life. Now it's time to give the telling of the story back to the author, who looks into my eyes. In order for you to forget me quickly, let me put this couplet, which I took out from the notes he kept about me on his desk, at the end of my story:

No belle lives in this city, O Nedim,

You saw a fairy – it is just your dream.

93

18

THE CUT-OFF TONGUE OF THE STORYTELLER TAHIR

Winter meant an early dusk for the Walled City. In the evenings, the city turned into a derelict dormitory awaiting its doom. The distance between man and his soul amplified. In that big gloomy house, wherever it reached, the eye would be trapped in an emptiness that kept on getting bigger and bigger. That emptiness was what attracted so many people to the city.

Storyteller Tahir, the warm heart of the city, sat in the inn, the entrance of which opened into the square. He tried to give life to the body of city in the long winter nights by sucking the bad blood out by his tongue. He brightened the embers of the big brazier with his stories. With his stories, he trickled drops of the elixir of warm summer days in the oil cans of the lamps that barely illuminated the large hall. The people sitting there would prick up their ears to the never-ending stories of this dervish of dreams. They would ride the horse of excitement and surprise travel to distant places, crossing the slopes of the night in a snap. The storyteller Tahir knew that there was a distant place in which everyone fell into and remained captivated. He led some men who could never find her themselves to a beautiful elusive woman, some to a heroism that would not taste defeat ever, some to treasures that never ended with any amount of spending, and some to unique traps. He had words with him with such charm that they shrunk the world. These were the words that compressed the world and put it in the palms of the listeners. People had no reason not to believe him in the desolation of the winter-ridden plain. If this good-humoured waterfall that poured dreams from its lips did not flow, it would be their lives they would blame rather than the stories he told. In the countless winter nights when the story turned into Tahir and Tahir turned into the story, what all had been spilled from his passionate tongue! He had drunk jugs full of water while he was telling the story of how the Lebanese Kurabi dried the Sayda River with his mouth and had once even drunk half of the Innkeeper Numan's earthenware water jar. He almost died coughing while he tried to save Gülbanu, daughter of the famous Carpetmaker Ziya from Isfahan, from tuberculosis and finally could continue further only after the Perfumer Yusuf's help. On his way to Kabul with Ferdowsi's hero, Rostam, he got out of breath and chose to take a break at a few stops to finish the story. While depicting the house of Mahinur, who fell in love with her husband every day afresh, he accidentally knocked the embers of the brazier into the hall of the inn and left the curiosity of his listeners burning until the embers were gathered. While trying to imitate the hanging of a Chinese spy in Herat, his breath was blocked for a while due to the rope wrapped around his neck. He could get the spy of Herat down from the gallows only with the help of his coughs. During the invasion of Gog and Magog, he hovered over the whole audience and Sherbet-maker Halil had to extend his slender neck in front of the invaders. While describing how the shoemaker's apprentice Vasif made shoes for the girl he had fallen in love with, he tore the stitches off his sandals and used his ill shaped fingers to show his audience the delicate feet of the girl. After the end of many of the stories he told his audience, Tahir had often gone inside his room in the inn, half-dead.

Tahir had a room in the inn. For people, he was just a man who started with his story and ended with his story. When all the knots of curiosity were untangled and the storyteller finished his word with a short prayer, Tahir also would be finished for the listeners. At the end of each story, they would go to their homes after gathering their cunning glances, unctuous smiles, and sleepy bodies. People wouldn't wonder who lived in the chest-cage of this great dreamer who was left alone in the large hall of the inn.

But Tahir himself wondered about it. One winter night, he suddenly asked himself, 'Who are you?' when he was returning to his room in the inn after finishing his tragic story of beautiful Honoriya, who was sent into exile by her king–brother because she fell in love with a servant who worked in the palace. He stood at the door for some time as he could not understand which part of him asked this question to which Tahir. He opened the door as an unanswered question, lit the lamp, went over to his bed, and pulled his glazed quilt over his head. He thought about the sleep that would come in some time as on other nights. But sleep did not come to him at all that night. The question that was stuck in his mind stood between him and his sleep and later swallowed his sleep. Swallowed his sleep, and got bigger, gradually.

'Who are you, who are you, who are you?' When the words that he spilled out of his tongue to please the people and the crowd that gathered around him are taken out of him, then actually no one was left. For a while he touched his hands and his beard that had started to turn white. He watched his body hesitantly, as if he was identifying it afresh and was looking for a suitable story for it. As he watched, he realized with horror that Tahir was just a scattered dream-house, each part of which became a part of the story that he told in the long winter nights – that's all!

The storyteller struggled to gather his own story all night long. He tried to heat the extinguished brazier with his childhood, but it didn't happen. He wanted to replace the last vestiges of the wick of the lamp with a bright day of his distant past. This too did not happen. Why, because while intending to decorate the dream-houses of this bored crowd, he distributed his experiences of both his past and future into his stories. The only thing remaining was a tongue, without an honour. In order to find the owner of his tongue, Tahir took out the contents of his own stories that were included with a different name in the countless stories he told, and spread them in front of him. First of all, he opened the contents of the story that made him a storyteller, for he considered it the heart of all his stories. The daughter of Carpetmaker Ziya from Isfahan, Gülbanu, who had tuberculosis, was none other than his beloved, who had become the reason for him to come to this city as he followed her, fearing that if he remained far from her, he would go mad.

Following the unfortunate fate of Gülbanu like a shadow, Ahmet from Isfahan changed his identity in the Walled City. First he became Tahir and later became Storyteller Tahir, who alleviated his suffering with the stories he told. However, each time he had been careful to keep the reason that brought Gülbanu to this city and his other life hidden under the new name, away from his stories. On one hand, he obviously wanted to be known by him; on the other hand, he wanted to prevent others from knowing him. Eventually, they both changed their names, they both became the city's favourites, and they were both doomed to live a lonely life surrounded by all the people. What upset Tahir most was that his beloved, about whom he told stories for decades while remembering his real name, did not indulge him even once. Who knows, perhaps, Gülbanu was uncomfortable in the presence of someone who knew her in this city and who had witnessed the twisted plots of her fate. Or, maybe even Gülbanu had forgotten that it was her, Gülbanu, just as she had forgotten that Ahmet was actually the young Ahmet of earlier times.

While tracing his stories, Tahir realized that it was of no use to think of the past. The years had lifted the barrier between reality and imagination, and had begun to convince the Storyteller to believe in what he recounted in his stories. After a while, every evening, he waited for the woman he loved to appear in his own story. Tahir had wiped out Ahmet from Isfahan and the stories had done the same to Tahir. The stories had not left an answer in him for his question, 'Who are you?' As he thought, Tahir saw that he would not be able to recollect the Storyteller, who was torn apart in pieces in the minds of countless men and in countless houses. He saw many Tahirs who stretched their heads on the cushions of the houses he had never entered, who sat in the halls of the inns he had never been to, who settled down near the braziers which never warmed up, and who embraced the women he never knew. All of them had not left a single piece of himself where he could stay. The only thing left from the people was his tongue, that treacherous and generous tongue. He made his decision. Next evening he intended to tell the story of Ahmet from Isfahan, which was swallowed by his stories earlier. Afterwards, he would give the only piece remaining in him away to the people. The small prayer at the end of his last story would be done by his cut-off tongue. He went to sleep and was asleep deep into the morning.

Those who came to listen to Tahir the next evening learned about the end that he chose for himself in a room of an inn, in the true language of the storyteller, for the first time.

19

METAPHOR OF THE MOUNTAIN

The people working in the palace of the Walled City were old and unemotional people, just like the palace itself. Time had erased the colours of those inside, blunted their desires, limited their emotions, weakened their joints, and above all, pushed them far away from the murmurings of people. The employees of the Walled City palace, who had lived there for years, spent their years as a government order, looked at life as a State edict, and spent the seasons as a State ceremony. The last governor of the city, Tuğluk, wanted to throw a stone into this still lake and cause some ripples. If he did not do this, the life of the water was going to end. Finally, he decided to insert fresh shoots into the old roots. He placed young court clerks in the rooms of the palace, which had lost their fervour and were left exhausted by the hundreds of seasons.

Each young clerk set out to work as a breakwater in the frosty sea of the State. The heavy sounds of the heel plates in their measured walks manifested themselves. In the already dry and cool marbles, the shadows of the bloody bodies began to play. After a long, dead-calm period, lively voices and cheerful laughter were heard in the wide hall of the palace. These young men with appetites made the meals, cauldrons, and the skilled chefs happy. The governor watched them from a distance. Each of them resembled an ivy that had just started to grow in a virgin forest. These young men did not have any clue about the length of the days or the shortness of the years. For some time, they were stuck between the rules of the palace and the happy-go-lucky attitude of their youth. Their fresh blood flowed unconsciously through the pages of the decrees. They were young, walking fast, jolting, and suddenly going far away in their imaginations while sitting down, making mistakes, joking, laughing, and talking a lot among themselves.

The governor understood them, mostly. They were right when they talked about the laws of the Principality. They would not deviate even by a grain of millet. They were committing mistakes, as mistakes shine the mirror of wisdom. They were laughing and guffawing because their chest cages were not yet surrounded by the bricks of years. They were going far in their imaginations, because in these times people always looked for themselves in far off places. All of these were, of course, natural. What was unnatural was the lightness of the words of these young clerks. They resembled sparrows, without a care in the world. They were jumping from one branch to another, playing games, but they could not make a small nest for themselves with the clay of two straws of truth. Love in their language resembled food cooked in a cold fire. They had become neither the fire nor a cauldron. While talking about bread, they were far away from the pain of a cracking seed. Old age was a crusted skin in their eyes and they felt the climate only with their words. And the young clerks were talking without pause. They were talking incessantly. They were forming a mountain with words and then they were also able to raze that mountain with just one word. How far they were from feeling the impending doom of the Principality!

One of the days when the summer sun was tiring the streets, the governor took his young clerks close to the high mountain near the Walled City. When they arrived precisely at the foot of the mountain, he summoned three of the most adventurous among them. He sent the first of them to the base of the mountain, the second to the middle, and the third to the summit of the mountain. And he ordered them, 'Look across from where you stand and bring us whatever your see from there.' The three clerks started walking towards the slopes that had been providing shadow to the city for hundreds of years.

The first one returned quickly. The governor said, 'Your path was short and the climb was not difficult. Tell me what you saw.'

The clerk said that he saw many trees, houses spread over the border of the city, a shepherd, and a flock of sheep over the slopes, when he looked across from where he stood. He noted down all the details one-by-one.

The second young clerk returned a little more tired than the first one. The governor said to him, 'You reached the middle of the mountain and the trouble you went through has dried your lips. Come on, tell us, what did you see across from where you were?' he asked.

The one who reached the middle said that he saw some villages, a river, and a small oak grove. He also described the details of what he saw.

It took much longer for the third young clerk to return. He could only descend from the summit long after it was dark. When the governor said, 'You are tired. You climbed to the summit and fought with the mountain. Yours was the longest road and the steepest slope. You came back a lot later than those two who went with you. Like the road, your burden must be heavy. Come on, pour the burden of your eyes and lighten up.'

The returned young clerk looked for words to speak. Then he gave the answer.

'I saw the entire city built in the middle of the plain, sir, but I could not catch any details that would connect the pieces. As if there was tulle (curtain) between us. From above, the houses of the city were like the helmets of an army spread across the plain.'

Tuğluk Bey looked at the clerks and smiled sadly. He said, 'You brought us both the knowledge of the summit and the signs of our doom. How few are the words of the one who climbs the heights.'

20

THE LAST SIGHT OF THE IMAGINED CITY

The magnificent army of the steppe

To reach Horasan,

Chose the shortest way for them.

Upon reaching the foot of a hill,

In the plains down below,

They saw a city taking a catnap.

They looked at it sharply,

It could not fight back no matter how much it wished.

'It melted, came untwined, and vanished

And the world forgot it.'

World Literature from STERLING⊒

The Street: A Novel

Hrishikes Bhattacharya
ISBN 978-93-86245-39-7

Pawada: A Novel

Wimaladasa Samarasinghe
ISBN 978-93-86245-67-0

Kalyug

Harsh Vardhan Wig
ISBN 978-93-86245-64-9

Life Wants to Live

Paola Martani
ISBN 978-93-86245-61-8

The Yin To My Yang

Jai Chaudhry
ISBN 978-93-86245-10-6

In the light of the path to know yourself
ZEN & SUFISM

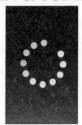

Ahmet Gűrbűz

STERLING⊒

mail@sterlingpublishers.in. • www.sterlingpublishers.in